Praise for
Speeding to Compassion

"As a personal friend, it's been amazing watching Connie Warden become a spectacular author and speaker! Her book *Speeding to Compassion* makes us look hard at our habits behind the wheel. Through her humor and storytelling, Connie guides us to better behavior. This is a great read!"

> —Keith Rennison, award-winning author of *Tenacity: You Don't Have to Get Lost in Nepal to Find Yourself, But it Helps*

"Connie Warden's generous heart and kind spirit make her not just a great storyteller and author, but also someone you want as a friend. Honest and deeply reflective, Connie presents a compelling case for embodying compassion in all of our affairs—with ourselves, others, and perhaps in one of the toughest places to exemplify this humble and soulful attribute...on the road. A relevant read, *Speeding to Compassion* has arrived at the perfect time in society where many not only seek, but are encouraged, to evade responsibility for their actions by placing blame on others. This quick and easy read will inspire you to be a mindful driver, a conscious human, and a considerate companion for your fellow travelers on the road of life."

> —Amanda McKoy Flanagan, LMSW, award-winning author of *Trust Yourself to Be All In*, and Intuitive Grief Coach

"Overall, *Speeding to Compassion* is a treasure trove of inspiration and laughter. Whether you need a gentle nudge towards kindness or simply an enjoyable read, this book is sure to leave a lasting impression. Highly recommended for anyone looking to uplift their spirits and enrich their life perspective!"

— Terri Mongait, award-winning author *Finding True Purpose*

"Connie M. Warden's love of ancient wisdom, modern science, and a mind-body connection led the author to develop her own yoga style and include it in her driving habits. Warden discusses how to be compassionate without losing your full range of emotions. You never know if the person you yell at or cut off in traffic could be someone who would have helped you later in the day or week. The people in your vehicle will appreciate your calmer disposition, too, as it's stressful to ride with an aggressive driver. Warden shows it is better to look at each situation in life and while driving with a few seconds of compassion than release negative emotions. Readers who are ready to take a calmer approach to driving will benefit from reading *Speeding to Compassion: Life Lessons and Humor to the Highroad*."

— Courtnee Turner Hoyle, Five Stars from Readers' Favorite

SPEEDING to
Compassion

LIFE LESSONS
AND HUMOR
FOR THE
HIGHROAD

Connie M. Warden, Dipl. Ac.

Speeding to Compassion: Life Lessons and Humor for the Highroad
Published by Well Being Warrior Press
Denver, CO

The events depicted in this book are authentic and all people are real. Dialogue is a representation of what was spoken based on the author's recollections. Names and many identifying details have been changed to protect the privacy of individuals. This book is not intended as a substitute for the medical advice of physicians or mental health professionals.

SELF-HELP / Personal Growth / Happiness
ISBN: 978-0-9963203-0-6

Cover and Interior Design by Victoria Wolf, wolfdesignandmarketing.com.

QUANTITY PURCHASES: Schools, companies, professional groups, clubs, and other organizations may qualify for special terms when ordering quantities of this title. For information, contact Connie Warden at Connie@conniewarden.com.

Well Being
WARRIOR
PRESS

Dedicated to Brett Warden. Through the many highs and the many lows, we continue to grow our souls.

CONTENTS

PART IV: THE MEDICINE IN THE HIGHROAD JOURNEY

PART I:

How It All Began

CHAPTER 1:

The Life-Changing
Five Seconds

"Never again; this is not the way I want to behave!"
—Connie

IT WAS 95 DEGREES OUTSIDE, sunny and not a cloud in sight.
A perfect day to be on or in a cool, relaxing body of water.

I loaded my blow-up paddleboard in the car and headed to a
quarry west of Denver, Colorado, to zen out. I love this quarry as
there are no motorboats, no loud engine noises, no smell of gasoline,
no booming music being blasted. Not that I don't enjoy loud music
at times, but today was reflection time, renewal time, so the serene
quiet was appealing. This was my self-care time to completely relax
and replenish my energy.

Maybe I'd even do some yoga on my paddleboard—time to slow
down and *be*. Ahhh, the slowness of paddling across the cool water,
the rhythm of paddling to the left, paddling to the right, pause, and
breathe. Inhaling the wonderful scent of the quarry, which smells
clean and reminds me of rain.

But I'm getting ahead of myself. I wasn't at the quarry yet.

I still had to *drive* to my "zen out" on this beautiful day.

Backing out of my driveway, I felt proud of myself for actually taking this time and not putting it off for another day (week/month/year). I rounded the corner at the end of my block with great expectations for my afternoon. I slipped on my sunglasses and could *feel* the smile on my heart. There was only one more turn between me and the road that would take me to the quarry.

The light turned green. The car in front of me didn't move—not even slightly.

This is where I went from "zen calm" to "Genghis Khan" in a few nanoseconds.

I beeped my horn madly and quickly swerved to the left, around this car that didn't seem to notice that the light had turned green. They clearly didn't care that their car was between me and my peace—even if the light had just turned green a nanosecond ago.

What the f*&k is their problem?!!

I honked my horn, spewing rage as I mumbled angry, trashy words about what a moron this driver *obviously* was and how they were too dangerous to be on the road and probably too old to be driving, anyway.

As I pulled up alongside the still-not-moving car, I glanced to my right to give the driver a "WTF?" look.

You *know* the look I'm talking about! The one we all give in hopes (irrationally) that it will actually benefit that driver—and help them drive like *us*. My heart dropped—because I instantly knew what was happening.

At the wheel, looking panicked, sat what appeared to be a teenage girl, the mother in the passenger seat.

Everything slowed down for me.

This was possibly the first time the young lady was out on the road learning to drive. I could see the terror in the girl's eyes as I passed. The kind of terror you see on screen at the *Halloween* movies. Her face was immobile with fear. You know the fight, flight, or freeze state when fear strikes. Well, this young girl was *frozen!*

Now, with the scene laid out in front of me and what I took in, I went back from Genghis Khan to Gandhi in three seconds.

It crushed my heart that I acted with such anger and had most likely caused her and her mother an untold amount of anxiety, fear, and stress.

So much for that "smile on my heart."

As quickly as I had gone from peaceful and excited, I slipped right into rage. And just as quickly from rage to shame. I had just been a real A-hole to a fellow human, and I was embarrassed at what a jerk I could be.

How could this happen so fast?

This was not the person I wanted to be.

Basically, I got caught up in road rage. This felt totally embarrassing to me. This was one of those experiences where I said to myself, "Never again; this is not the way I want to behave!"

My behavior that day was a complete disconnect for me. Here I was, practicing and teaching yoga and meditation—trying to cultivate inner peace and vitality. I felt like a fake.

This experience changed the trajectory of my life.

Reflection Drive

While driving the rest of the way to the quarry I could feel in my body the tension of disbelief, shame, and disgrace. It was hard for me to take a deep breath.

Fortunately, all the work I had done to that point in my life to cultivate presence, peace, and calm—and stop the voice of my inner critic, which is the voice of the superego, from taking over—allowed me to put those feelings away until I got on the water. More importantly, I was bringing in (barely, but just enough) self-compassion for my actions.

I can't even explain how distraught I was at my behavior.

The potential to massively beat myself up was clearly available, but I chose not to explore this behavior until I arrived at the quarry. The beauty and calm of the quarry, and the freedom of my paddleboard, would give me the space to hold and look at my experience with more self-compassion. Until then, I turned on some music to relax my mind and stop the inner critic.

It wasn't easy, but I kept this voice at bay until I was out on the water.

The Concept of the Mindful, Kindful Driver Was Born

I finally arrived at the quarry. As I pumped up my paddleboard, I suddenly had this flashback to a time in my twenties. I remember feeling (just a little) superior to one of my younger sisters when she told me this story.

Not too long after she had gotten her driver's license, she was stopped at a red light, the first car in line to go when the light turned green. The light turned green and my sister sat there, unaware, caught up in some distraction.

At some point, the car behind her beeped. She immediately put up her right hand and gave the driver the finger. A nice F-U to *that* driver.

So, the driver put on the patrol car's lights and the siren and pulled her over. The police officer was kind and wanted to point out to her that there are good and appropriate uses of the car horn.

I would never be so quick to rage. Or so I thought at that time.

Forty years later, I'm eating humble pie. Hey, sis, I get ya! Hey, reader, I get ya! Oh, the irony. Another gentle (well, maybe not gentle) reminder of how feelings of superiority almost always come back at us.

While floating on the paddleboard, I decided I was going to figure out a path to be a more mindful, kindful driver. I had paddled over to the other side of the quarry, where I was the only person around. I lay face down on my paddleboard, my left hand drawing circles and figure eights in the water, the sun warming my back at the same time that a slight breeze cooled it. I was feeling peaceful, kind, compassionate.

Why couldn't I be peaceful, kind, and compassionate *all the time*? Especially while driving?

I made the decision that I was going to change. I was going to stop being a toxic driver. (More about what I mean by "toxic" driving in Chapter 2.) I would work on becoming a more mindful, kindful driver *regardless of how other people were driving*.

THAT was the person I wanted to be.

To my credit, I wasn't a raging driver *all* the time. However, after what I experienced that day, I knew I could do better. My rage had exposed a part of me, a very human part, that can get ugly angry when inconvenienced.

Through years of practicing mindfulness and meditation, I have become aware and able to recognize these human qualities (like anger, rage, jealousy, and passive-aggressiveness). But **none of us, myself included, should become aware of the uglier sides of the human experience without also learning to refrain from shaming ourselves for being human.**

I have learned to experience these feelings without necessarily creating a narrative, as I first did with the girl I frightened. The narrative that someone, somehow, was deliberately trying to keep me from my peace and pleasure.

Through this journey of becoming a mindful, kindful driver, and using my mindfulness trainings and practices, I have learned to acknowledge my anger, rage, jealousy, and the occasional foray into passive-aggressiveness; and to accept these feelings for what they are— the human experience. I haven't, by any means, mastered this ability. In fact, I think it's a lifelong practice, but I am getting closer to keeping outside events from fully taking over my thoughts and actions. I am still on this journey, and I am looking forward to sharing it with you.

Why a whole book on the subject?

I believe my story is a universal story, and will ultimately help people be kinder to themselves and kinder to the whole of humanity and the natural world.

My endeavor has led me to have more self-compassion with my not-so-lovely, but very human, qualities. And I believe, when we can accept our own "ugliness," we can have more compassion for others' ugliness. More compassion for humanity as a whole. If I'm going to do any speeding, I want it to be toward compassion.

CHAPTER 2:
The Disconnect

"We are, at all times, cultivating our human/
spiritual traits. Positively, or not!"

—Connie

AS MOST OF US KNOW, our inner critic can get super busy when
we have a disconnect between how we *want* to behave and how we
actually behave.

I was experiencing *cognitive dissonance*. This is the psychological
tension that happens and is created when a person's behavior is not
consistent with their thoughts and beliefs.

I came across this quote shortly after I started my mindfulness
journey and completely related to it:

> You may indeed exemplify kindness in how you treat your chil-
> dren and your grandmother ... But if you honk your horn in
> red-faced anger at a slow-moving grandmother who's taking her
> grandchildren to school, then you're way, way, out of balance.

—Dr. Wayne W. Dyer

Sometimes, I was waaaayyyy out of balance. The stress of driving, every day—especially the driving that was between me and my moments of self-care—was the epitome of the disconnect between me and how I wanted to behave in life.

I really wanted to figure out **how to maintain a peaceful mindset**, be a kind and thoughtful driver—even when there are so many drivers out there who are not. Even though there are a lot of crazy, stupid, idiotic—even dangerous—things drivers do. Like me, that day.

Could I take that wonderful peacefulness I felt floating on the lake and maintain it in other situations? Situations where I was *not* on a lake?

If you, dear reader, can relate to any of this, I want to encourage you to put your hands on your heart and find that part of you that can offer yourself some compassion for being human. (I will be talking more on self-compassion later.)

I want to share what I've learned through years of personal and spiritual growth. It will help you to understand the whole reasoning behind this compassionate and mindful journey of mine and the lens I am using.

What Are We Cultivating?

We cultivate certain traits throughout our lives, consciously or not. What we do, think, and say, *consistently*, is what we are cultivating.

Here is a list of a few traits we could be cultivating. I have them in two categories, but they make up the whole of a human being. I'm having a little fun with the "Zen Calm" and the "Genghis Khan" because I want there to be some lightness on this journey. One side could be perceived as extremely negative. But these are our medicines to help cultivate the positive (more to come on understanding our medicine). So how can they be negative? Again, a universal experience among us humans.

"Yes, And" Table

Zen Calm	Genghis Khan
Love	Impatience
Joy	Jealousy
Compassion	Hatred
Inner Wisdom	Vengeance
Patience	Rage
Basic Goodness	Anger
Big-Heartedness	Greed
Equanimity	Judgment
Useful Power	Destructive Power
Worthiness	Unworthiness
Trust	Insecurity
Self-Referral	Object Referral

One of the great paradoxes in life is we are both/and. Which is why this table has the title that it does. We *all* have soulful qualities *and* human qualities.

The Desire to Be Genuine and Wholehearted

Understanding and cultivating our soul qualities of love, compassion, grace, and so on, cannot be learned at the library or in a book. It is experienced in the body, like all emotions. Which is why I am bringing in the mindfulness concept.

Ultimately, I wanted to take full responsibility for my behavior. I didn't want to feel like a fake. You know those people—do as I say, not as I do. It's disingenuous, and I was, and always will be, endeavoring to be a person who is genuine and wholehearted (not hard-hearted).

Here is a story you most likely have heard, yet the repetition is so grounding. There are many, many versions from many cultural backgrounds, revolving around a wise elder and his grandson. The grandfather tells his grandson about the two wolves we all have within us. One of these wolves is competitive and greedy, full of anger, impatience, and jealousy. The other is full of love, compassion, goodness, and joy. They are always fighting for our attention, for our willingness to make one of them dominant.

The grandson asks, "Grandfather, which one of them wins?"

The grandfather says, "It depends on which one you feed."

It feels like it should be easier to get along with everyone. Even while driving. I think you would agree with me that being in a human body going around on this ball we call Earth is not easy.

Why is it so hard?!

I believe driving can be one of the hardest places to cultivate that good wolf because there is nothing humanizing about it. We are all surrounded by these steel-caged shells, going at speeds that don't make our bodies feel good or even natural, with our own agendas, and not recognizing we are dealing with other humans.

I'm going to add here another incentive for cultivating compassion while driving, even though it *is* so hard.

Two clinical psychologists, Dr. Stan Steindl and Dr. James Kirby, who founded the Compassion Initiative, say, "There is nothing inherently wrong with anger as an emotion, but nowhere is anger less helpful, more common, and potentially more dangerous than when we are behind the wheel of a car."

I talk more about my "why" for this journey in Part II, but for now, one important reason to cultivate more compassion while driving is simply for our safety.

One Itty, Bitty Sentence Transforms My Life?

I've been an observer all of my life. I came into this world as an observer and a discoverer. When I'm learning something new, I feel the most alive. Especially if that something new expands my human and spiritual capacity. However, being an observer can also make one feel not connected (like an outsider) to the world.

I grew up with seven brothers and sisters and a one-parent income. One of the few times we could indulge in anything was how many books we could take out at the library.

I had, and still have, this insatiable curiosity about almost any subject. By the time I was seven years old, I absolutely delighted in opening any drawer—eeny, meeny, miny, moe—of the library card catalog (I'm dating myself here), going through the cards, and seeing what caught my eye, what was going to pique my curiosity that day. The thought that I could learn more about anything still has that feeling of aliveness for me.

I was still going to the library, meandering through the aisles and stacks of books to bring home, when I began to drive at sixteen years old. Reading was one of the best ways I could enjoy my summer vacation. That, and reading books at a beach by the many lakes where I grew up in Wisconsin.

That summer, I brought a book on yoga home to peruse. One sentence in the book set my direction for the rest of my life.

This yoga book stated that **the body needs to be flexible to help the mind be flexible.**

That may sound trite, but for me, it was more like I looked up, the clouds parted, and angels began to sing and play the trumpets. *That's* what that sentence did for me.

The idea of the mind and body being connected just fascinated me! I wanted to be a person who was open-minded, willing to learn and grow. It was my first taste of the philosophy behind mind-body connection. I wanted to understand more.

At the time of this epiphany, I felt like I was living in a crazy whirlwind of a household. My dad's tendency to anger, my mother's bouts of depression, and all the turmoil that seven other siblings could create in a four-bedroom, 1400-square-foot house drove me further into my books and finding hiding places where I would be left alone. Not that things were always crazy; there was also a lot of love. Which I will always have fond memories of. Love and craziness.

The Gap Between My Practices and Using Them in Real Life

Today, I'm an acupuncturist, meditation and yoga instructor, and serial entrepreneur.

What good would my practices be if I was mindful while sitting on a cushion in my living room, yet I didn't genuinely behave with mindful attention when I was out in the world?

Another way to say this is that if my practice didn't leave me able to show up in a mindful state when I left the house, if the practice only allowed me to be mindful when I was all alone, it wasn't a useful practice.

So how could I apply my practices of yoga, meditation, mindfulness, and martial arts (more to come about my martial arts practices)—which are all about mind and body harmony—to the area of driving? *This* was my journey!

My Yoga and Meditation Practice

At sixteen years old, I started my yoga practice from that first yoga book. In the beginning, I stared at the pictures and read the content as if I were looking into a new, exotic world. Every few days, I looked at the poses with a sense of awe and started to imitate them.

They allowed me to stretch. I found that I just loved to stretch my body. In fact, it almost became an obsession.

At that time, I was living with my family and siblings in a tri-level house. The open staircase led from the kitchen to the top level of the house, where there were three bedrooms. There was a banister at the top of the stairs such that you could reach over it and pick up the phone that was on the kitchen wall below.

That phone was my connection to my friends, and like most teenagers, I was often on the phone. The phone had a long cord and could even reach the steps to the bedrooms from the kitchen. I hung out on those steps with the corded phone and did yoga poses while chatting with my friends. I even managed to do splits. One foot on the first step, the other on the fourth step.

Or I would raise my hands over my head, bending side to side. Or somehow do dancer's pose, my shoulder holding the phone to one ear.

As I mentioned, I have seven brothers and sisters. Each one of them is more of a smartass than the next one. They had a ball giving me a lot of crapola for what must have afforded them plenty of material: me stretching as much as I could while somehow avoiding pulling that phone off the kitchen wall.

Most of the time, having them make fun of me was enough to stop me from doing something (or give them a view of one of my fingers). But my love of stretching (which is also about being present) overrode my embarrassment. I simply didn't care. I continued without batting an eye to be in dancer's pose if I felt like it.

Now, many years later, I am grateful to that girl I once was who risked embarrassment by following her instincts and doing something that must have seemed ridiculous to this family of smartasses living in Wisconsin in the 1970s. She set me up for a lifetime of exploration in an area of wellness that is common now but wasn't so common back then. Forty years later, I have taken many classes in many styles of yoga from teachers with plenty of diverse lenses (Bikram, Iyengar, Ashtanga, Yin, Restorative, Kundalini), as well as teacher certifications, to discover my own style. A style that allows me to feel as authentic on the yoga mat as I feel on a meditation cushion or behind the wheel of my vehicle.

Through the years, my motivation for my yoga practice has changed. It started out as a way to understand the mind/body connection and the wisdom of this connection. Then it went to having the best posture, the best balance, and being extreme in my flexibility. Finally, it morphed into more of a meditation style. And guess what—I call it "Mindful, Kindful Yoga."

There are so many styles and purposes of yoga. Here is my definition of what yoga means for me today (and why it was helpful on this driving journey).

Yoga poses are not the goal. Becoming flexible is not the goal.
The goal is to make it to your mat.
To remember this is your sacred time.
To connect to the wisdom of your mind, and also the mental noise it can create.

To connect to the wisdom of your heart, and all its protective hardness.

To be in awe of your body and the wisdom it contains.

To slow the breath and the mind and to remember what is real.

To remember this is your special time for self-inquiry.

To build the tools that make your life off the mat as sacred as the time on the mat.

I believe that our hearts' desires for ourselves will also have an effect *beyond* ourselves. Indeed, I believe that as we aim to be more heartful and open, these aspects can spread out on the web of life that connects us all, and all of those around us benefit. I will talk more about what is called, "the wake we leave behind" in a bit. Leaving a wake of kindness is my aim, every day.

Driving was going to give me the opportunity to expand my compassion and my heart. Again, driving as my medicine to put into practice what I focus on while on the yoga mat *into real life*.

From Business School to Acupuncture College
When I first went to college in my late teenage years, I studied Business, because that is what everyone around me told me was my best option at the time. I had a long way to go before I learned to listen to my gut, to what resonated with me, rather than what those around me thought *should* resonate with me. As a result, I got my undergraduate degree in BS (wink, wink)—Bachelor of Science in Business and Finance.

Years later, with two kids in grade school and me a stay-at-home mom—at least some of the time—I went back to school for my

Masters in Oriental Medicine (M.OM), also known as Traditional Chinese Medicine (TCM) or acupuncture.

The turning point for me to attend graduate school was the recognition, the awareness, of how much I loved yoga and what the whole-body awareness of mind, body, and spirit meant to me. I was always wanting to learn more.

Just as yoga opened up the possibility of physical and mental vitality and flexibility, TCM took things further; it expanded on my love for whole-body awareness—awareness of the mind, body, and spirit as a whole system.

For much of my life, I resonated with various Eastern philosophies. Not only the practices of yoga and martial arts—which I will get to—but even the practice of Chinese brush painting, which I love.

What I really loved then, and still love, is combining ancient wisdom together with modern science in order to live a life filled with vitality, joy, and love—a life of wholeness. So much scientific research is coming out to prove and validate alternative and indigenous medicine systems. So exciting!

Now, if I just learn to drive with vitality, joy, and love ....

Driving as My Medicine

My newfound goal became to let driving be my medicine to stay compassionate to my imperfect humanness. To others' imperfect humanness.

What does "driving as my medicine" really mean? Medicine is meant to heal something that doesn't feel good. Sometimes that medicine is darn bitter. Not pleasant.

Driving with anger and rage, and staring people down is toxic driving. Unhealthy, unwholesome, and noxious. I was going to use driving—this bitter medicine—to help me understand the unhealthy disconnect in my behavior.

I remember listening to a podcast on leadership, and the speaker was a manager of a large corporation. He retold a story about getting ready to park his car one morning at his office. It was a cold, dreary morning. The wind was such that the misty rain flew into your face as you entered the building. He saw a lone parking spot still available close to the building and aimed for it. Just as he arrived, a young man suddenly pulled in front of his car, cutting him off. Shocked, the manager slammed on his brakes, then backed up and drove to find another parking spot.

After the manager arrived at his office and settled in, he asked his administrative assistant to let in the first person scheduled to be interviewed that day. I think you know what happened next. Lo and behold, it was the young man who had cut him off to get the parking spot. Needless to say, the young man did *not* get the job. The manager actually explained why to him.

The idea that, if you are a bully driver, you are probably going to be a bully employee. Now that is some bitter medicine. You acted like a jerk, and it came back at you.

"How you do one thing is how you do everything" is a saying that hits home for me.

I *may* have been that driver once. Screaming around the parking lot corner to beat the other person who I know wanted that parking spot as bad as me. Today, in order to keep myself from becoming competitive, I park as far away as possible so I can stay relaxed and calm. This practice keeps me from my worst tendencies, and I get the added benefit of increasing my walking steps.

I call myself a "well-being warrior" because I'm so interested in the expansion of our human potential and how the mind-body connection is used for this path.

And if you are on this path, dear reader, you know it takes warrior-like energy to stick with it. The transformation process of expanding our potential takes grit, effort, commitment, and self-love.

Now that you understand how my journey started, and I hope you related to some of it, I'm going to talk about the benefits of being a more compassionate driver. Thanks for joining me on the journey to the highroad.

PART II:

Mindful, Kindful Driving Is Literally Good for Us

CHAPTER 3:

The Power of Our Thoughts on Our Body

*"Being a more mindful and compassion-
ate driver will always benefit one's health."*
—Connie

ULTIMATELY, THIS JOURNEY on earth is about our physical, mental, and spiritual health.

I explained a little about why I started this quest to become a more mindful, kindful driver and, ultimately, a more compassionate person toward myself and others. A desire to close that gap between how I wanted to be as a human and how I was really behaving while driving.

Also, closing that gap is healthier, more genuine, and a big-hearted way to live. Being more mindful and compassionate will always benefit one's health, whether physical, mental, or spiritual. These health benefits were my "why," and helped me stay strong in my goal. Especially when I would find myself going backward at times. Meaning, driving more toxically than not.

All Activity That Happens in the Head
Causes Activity in the Body

We all know our thoughts are powerful and that they powerfully affect our bodies and physical health. And most of you know that close to 90 percent of our thoughts are subconscious, lacking the awareness we are even thinking them. Often called: autopilot.

Mindfulness is a way to become *aware* of the thoughts and thought patterns that cause us harm. The activity going on in my head while driving, a lot of the time, was not promoting my health. Nor is it promoting to yours.

The narratives in our head can harmonize our body-mind or can cause disharmony. Thoughts can cause ease or dis-ease. All activity in the head (conscious or not) causes activity (physiologically) in the body.

Imagine you are driving along a quiet, two-lane road among farms with miles of green grass, and large, expansive, verdant trees. Suddenly, you round a corner and see a truly magnificent sunset. You automatically go into a state of awe. You pull over to sit and admire the golden light mixed with shades of pink and purple on the clouds, and the big yellow ball sinking toward the horizon. You think to yourself about how lucky you are, how absolutely grateful you are to catch this sunset. Those words and feelings cause many wonderful physiological chemicals to be released into your body, allowing you to feel relaxed and joyful.

The opposite is true as well.

Complaining, beating yourself up, finding the worst in everything, complaining (second time for emphasis) are all ways to dump physiological chemicals into your body and cause tension, lower the immune system, impact the nervous system, and all the other systems in our body in response to chronic stress. *This* is what I mean by toxic driving!

The following are some personal and collected examples of the power of our thoughts and how they can affect us physically.

Constipation—Words Have Power

There was a lady that I knew briefly, and she would say "no shit" upwards of fifty times a day.

A little bit of an exaggeration ...

Me: Hi, nice to meet you.

Her: No shit, nice to meet you too.

Me: You have a beautiful garden.

Her: No shit, thank you.

Me: Looks like you have a lot of experience with gardening. So many veggies.

Her: No shit, been doing this for twenty years.

Me: Could you help me with my garden?

Her: No shit, would love to.

Would you be surprised that she had a challenge with constipation? She wasn't a client of mine, so I didn't say anything. Of course, her constipation could have been caused by many other factors. But it didn't surprise me that she had this issue because of the consistent use of her words and, presumably, her thoughts.

Our mental thoughts affect our physical health, as simple as that. Such is the power of words.

Hip Pain—Beliefs Have Power

I worked with a man who was in his late fifties and came to me for acupuncture and massage due to pain in his right hip. "My dad had hip pain, which is why I'm sure I have hip pain." He believed that this hip pain was genetic.

Maybe, maybe not.

I said I believed he in fact did *not* have to have this pain (I felt it was 100 percent due to muscle tension) just because his father had, and I talked a bit about epigenetics. Epigenetics is the study of how our lifestyles (our behaviors, beliefs, diet, and environment) can cause changes that affect the way our genes work. The way our genes are expressed.

He eventually realized that telling himself his hip pain was due to genetics from his father had become something of a mantra (and a deep belief) for some time now.

We had two more sessions to relieve his hip pain, and he didn't need to come back. His pain was gone. He even said he finally believed he could be free from hip pain, and he stopped unconsciously telling himself this genetic story. He never came back to me for hip pain. We kept in touch, and years later, he still had no pain.

Such is the power of belief.

Skipped Heartbeats—The Environment Has Power

I was working with "Anna" for the third time with acupuncture and massage. She was in her mid-twenties and what I would call a rather "self-aware" person. Among other things, she wanted to lower the effects of stress on her body and mind with massage and acupuncture. I was very surprised, then, to feel her pulses on this third treatment. About every third beat was a missed beat. She was being monitored by her MD as this was a known issue. But the missed heartbeat being monitored was every twentieth beat. I recommended that she go see her MD regarding this change.

She then revealed to me she was having big-time problems with her relationship and was thinking of separating. Although this helped explain her stress level and, therefore, the possibility that this was causing the frequency of the missed heartbeats, I still wanted her to check this out with her MD.

I saw her again two weeks later. She did not go to see her doctor; instead, she decided to end her relationship and moved into her own apartment. Her pulses, her heartbeat, had come back to normal.

Such is the power of a healthy environment. Why do you think crime rates go down when community gardens are put in? Why do crime rates go down when a community is cleaned up? Our environment matters to our mental health.

Driving, for the most part, is not a healthy environment. Many of us can't break up with driving. Which is indeed the crux of this book: how do we deal with this non-healthy environment? I will be sharing tips and tricks at the end of this book. If you want to start your journey to the highroad right now, go ahead and take a sneak peek. Go to Part V: Various Valuable Techniques to Stop the Damn Stories and Steer You to the Highroad. (I know, it's a very long subtitle, but I like it.) Peruse the list, pick one that jumps out at you, and start your journey today.

Body Tension and Our Health

First of all, how do we get tension in our bodies? Where does it come from and why? We of course need *some* tension in our muscles so we can have strength, stand and move, or we would be noodles.

I'm talking about the consistent tension patterns we've built up through the years as a form of protection.

Being in a job that brings on tension (because you hate it).

Being in a relationship that doesn't grow your soul.

Or consistently being tense while driving.

This habitual tension can become hardened and difficult for us to release.

When he found out what I was writing a book about, the husband of a friend of mine told me about the body tension he carried from driving. Years back, when he was in California, he had to drive almost an hour each way for his job. When he finally didn't need to do that commute every day, he realized how much tension had left his body. He said it felt like it took two more weeks to feel fully relaxed.

Tension affects the posture of our body, including our face. It can affect our physiology, our pain levels, and, quite frankly, our happiness. Again, knowing something about the negative effects of tension, as I did from my acupuncture and massage schooling, didn't stop me from tensing up while driving and deeming others idiots.

I want to share a few stories about tension patterns. Why? Because we most likely are exacerbating them in our cars while driving. **And we don't have to do this.**

Grouper Fish Pose Handed Down for Generations

Like many people during the pandemic, I had a lot of online meetings. At one point I realized, with much dismay, that I was doing that jaw-jutting thing that I've seen in pictures throughout generations of my family. It's not a good look, dear reader. It looks like a cross between anger, annoyance, and indignation. Nope, not a pretty look. I call it the Grouper fish pose. Most varieties of Groupers have that lower jaw extending out beyond the upper jaw. They look crabby and mad (and constipated).

I then began the endeavor to "catch" myself—in other words, bring in awareness —when I was in Grouper fish pose and to simply relax my jaw. I realized that my jaw position also stressed my neck, and I had to consciously relax my neck.

THEN! One day I was talking with one of my sisters, and she started complaining about what was going on in the office where she works. There it was! Her jaw started jutting out! The more she talked about the goings-on at her work the more her jaw protruded out, till—I swear—her jaw was four inches from her body. I was totally astonished. For so many reasons.

- One, that she didn't notice it. (Which I didn't point out— not the time or place, if you know what I mean.)
- Two, that this has been passed down for generations.
- Three, *Crap, I'm sure I look just like her when driving* (madly).
- Four, I really need to work on this myself!

This tension pattern was certainly one I imitated from my dad, and ancestors for generations. It is easily done.

In massage school, we watched a short film on posture. What stuck out to me at the time, and what I will always remember most, was this father and his five-year-old son walking away from the camera and up a grassy hill. The father had some type of injury and was walking with a limp. **And so was his son.** He was simply imitating his father's walk. Yikes!

Can you think of a tension or habitual pattern you may have generated from imitating other adults? Are they patterns you want to keep?

Who Is That Person?

My neighborhood was having their annual summer block party. The street was blocked off, and the neighbors were setting up tables and chairs, getting ready for the food and drinks. I looked around and saw a lady I didn't know. I had been living on this block for over two decades. And when I say "block," I mean our street really is only one city block long, and we all know each other since most of us have spent two or three decades living there.

As I watched this unknown lady, I noticed something familiar about her. Ahh, she had to be the mother of my neighbor two doors down. She had the exact same posture as her daughter. I recognized this lady solely based on her posture.

In the same way that my family has produced habitual tension patterns regarding jaw-jutting, tension can produce ways that we stand and move our bodies. This tension may be the result of not just the way we may have imitated our parents' postures, but ways we **may have adopted stiff, inflexible thought patterns.**

Where Tension Comes From (beyond the Family)

Starting from childhood, we all have done various things to protect ourselves from a world that is sometimes pretty darn harsh. What may surprise you is muscle tension actually helps to protect us from the mean words we may hear, the heartbreak we feel.

At some point, that tension is going to cause us problems and may not be useful any longer.

When we are going to be late for work and thinking how it may negatively affect our day, we harden. When we see someone hurting an animal or a child, we harden. When we repeatedly go over a bad conversation in our head, we harden. When we yell at the referee during a bad call and scream at the TV screen, we harden. When we get angry at stupid drivers, we harden. We are simply being toxic to our bodies.

All the negative things we say to ourselves, that relentless inner critic, causes tension and fatigue.

When we think of someone we love, our bodies soften. When we see a spectacular sunset, we soften. When someone gives us a compliment, we soften. When we admire someone's courage, we soften.

Take a guess: what do most of us humans do more of? Soften or harden?

You are right if you think we do more hardening, more protecting. Our poor nervous system doesn't get a break. Our muscles don't get a break.

Another way to say this pattern is, we are charging our nervous system (hardening) or discharging (softening). We need both, but, once again, are we in balance with both or do we consistently do more charging of our nervous system, causing consistent tension?

Consistent muscle tension = lack of
blood supply = numbness.

Consistent charging of our nervous system
= stress on all our body systems.

We Experience Life through Our Bodies

But this is how we experience life—in our bodies!

Joseph Campbell, a writer and professor of mythology and the human experience, said, "I don't think people are really seeking the meaning of Life. I think we're seeking an experience of being alive ... we want to feel the rapture of being alive."

One definition of rapture is "a **feeling** of intense pleasure or joy."

Not if our body is numb, though.

I often reference *The Wisdom of the Enneagram*, a book that uses a diagram called the Enneagram as a tool for self-understanding. The authors, Don Richard Riso and Russ Hudson, suggest that we work with the body because the "body is always here in the present .... Therefore, if we are aware of the sensations of our bodies, it is a **solid piece of evidence that we are present** (emphasis added)."

We experience our lives, ourselves, through our senses. What we feel, taste, smell, and hear. Love is felt, joy is felt, anger is felt, contentment is felt—in the body.

Prolonged tight muscles become weak and numb.

Right now, dear reader, close your eyes (after reading this sentence) and take three long, slow, deep breaths, followed by three very relaxing, softening, releasing exhales. Notice what parts of the body relax.

You could do this a thousand times a day, and each time, you would notice a muscle group that didn't need to be tensed. It's a habitual tension pattern. We all have them. We all think—we all feel.

Again, from *The Wisdom of the Enneagram*: "Conscious relaxation is a matter of learning how to come back to the here and now again and again, opening up to a deeper and deeper impression of reality."

This is also the point of mindfulness training.

Riso and Hudson go on to say that when our muscle tension is consistent and prolonged, "We no longer feel our body." And "as long as we are not feeling these tensions, they are not going to be released, and they eventually wear down our health and vitality." Wow! This is why I wanted to make changes to my driving habits.

The Hamster Wheel of Tension and Pain

Someone with a great deal of pain, especially for a long period of time, is going to naturally have a lot of muscle tension. That's the cycle of pain. Pain -> causes tension -> which causes more pain -> which causes more tension.

I had a new client come into my office and announce, slowly and lethargically, "I'm here because my wife made this appointment." I can't say these are my favorite types of patients, but I wasn't deterred.

I didn't go down a mental path of trying to "prove" to him that acupuncture might indeed benefit him. I stayed curious and open-minded about what was going to result from his treatment.

He was walking slowly and had pain written all over his face. Clearly, he wasn't happy. Either being at this appointment, or generally in life.

His back pain was so bad that he had to take a leave of absence from his work. He was one unhappy person, and clearly, his wife was fed up.

Luckily for him, his body really took to the acupuncture, and after three treatments he was able to go back to work. He only needed two more treatments after that and I didn't see him again. The difference in his disposition and his personality between his first and third appointment was dramatic. So much less pain, so much less tension.

The point is:

1. We all have tension patterns we grew up with or create.
2. Tension can equal stuck-ness, pain, and disharmony.
3. With awareness, we can release and transform these patterns—even while driving—to make us happier humans.

Like many of the stories I've told, our thoughts affect our bodies and can give us so much information—but only when there is conscious awareness.

As I've read about these ideas, I've realized that the activity most likely to produce jaw-jutting and other forms of tension and hardness, for me, was driving. I knew I could be better to myself, to my health and vitality, by not being a tensed-up version of myself.

The moral of the story for all of us is: body tension and pain wreak havoc on one's life. Don't add to it by smack-talking when driving.

This awareness is both a tough and a simple thing to accomplish. We'll talk more in Part III on what you can do to break this cycle. First, let's look at mental and spiritual health, and the effects of tension.

CHAPTER 4:
Joyride for the Mind

"Master your mind, master your life."
—Magnus Steele

IN CASE YOU HAVEN'T GUESSED IT, *Speeding to Compassion* is a journey to help us become happier and healthier human beings. Without our personal health and happiness, it is hard to maximize our human and spiritual potential.

Our thoughts and narratives going on in our minds play a critical role in our health and happiness.

Squeezing the Cactus

Really, what I'm doing when I'm cussing and raging on the road is what is called "stupid suffering."

What is stupid suffering? It's like squeezing a cactus. Who would do that? It's going to hurt!

Screaming at the TV because the referee made a bad call is stupid suffering. It's not going to change the call, and there will always be bad calls.

Raging at other people is stupid suffering. I'm poisoning my body with chemical neurotransmitters that tense my body, lower my immune system, stress my nervous system, and more, as was mentioned in Chapter 3. Toxic driving is stupid suffering.

Here's Connie Squeezing the Cactus

I'm driving with my husband, who is in the passenger seat, and I'm concerned about not getting to our destination on time.

Then, I am waiting to turn right, but I have to wait for a young woman who has a cane and is slowly limping to the other side of the street.

I have to *wait*!

"OMG, if she would have just taken care of herself, I wouldn't have to be waiting here," I cry out!

How uncompassionate is that? I even knew *at the time I was saying it* that it was a stupid and inconsiderate thing to think and speak.

But then I started to laugh, and so did my husband. Stupid suffering at its finest.

I hope you can see how we all do this stupid suffering stuff. We humans, we are all in this together... and yet, if one wants to stop squeezing the cactus, it will take some mindfulness.

Can you, dear reader, think of some ways you squeeze the cactus? Something you may not really need to say or think that may be a habitual pattern? Stay tuned for mindfulness practices that are helpful in stopping this.

Athletes Train More than Their Bodies

It's important for athletes to be able to train their minds as well as their bodies. My sixteen-year-old niece is training and expanding her basketball skills. She wants to make it onto her high school varsity team and eventually play in college. Last summer, her basketball camps were mostly about *mindset*.

If they miss a basket or a free throw they can't afford to spend minutes being upset about it. They have to let it go and stay in the present moment. Thinking about the past is not going to help you moving forward in this fast-moving game.

Let's pick a slow-moving game. How about golf? I'm all too familiar with this one, as my husband has been playing golf since he was five years old, and I began to learn the game from him thirty-five years ago.

In golf, you will hit "bad" shots. The ball goes left, goes right, lands in the water or the sand trap. It happens to the best of them, even the pros. In my case, most of my shots are not that great. If you want to play golf, and enjoy it, the ability to let go of a bad shot is a must.

All professional athletes train their minds for the game they love to play.

We are training our minds anyway, consciously or unconsciously.

Can we all train our minds so we can enjoy life, the game of life? There are many ways to do this, and right now, I'm using driving to train my mind.

Martial Arts—Another Way I Practiced Mind-Body Harmony

Another one of my self-care practices was training in various martial arts. I tried one martial arts class at the local YMCA when I was seventeen years old. Maybe I went on the wrong day, but it felt like the focus was on beating people up. Not on becoming disciplined or a way to become a stronger person. I was not interested.

When I first started college, one of the people in the co-op where I lived was a student and a teacher of Aikido. I tried it and loved it! I appreciated the philosophy behind this martial art. Aikido is translated as "The Way of Harmony." And, like yoga, the practice is about becoming better in body, mind, and spirit. I really resonated with the philosophy behind it.

Aikido is said to be a path to refining **the body** through balance, flexibility, and coordination; refining the **mind** through focus, self-confidence, and awareness; and refining the **spirit** through grounding, being positive, and feeling peaceful. What an awesome thing to practice in real life. Maybe even while driving?

I practiced Aikido for over five years. I practiced at several *dojos* (martial art schools) when I moved to Colorado and then eventually found another dojo that practiced a combination of martial arts that I will share later.

A Rigid Body Is Easily Manipulated

Through my years of various martial arts, I've learned that people who have more tension and constriction in their bodies are more easily manipulated. Stiff, rigid bodies (and often minds also, as you will see below) are easier to maneuver on the dojo mat. And I'm also translating this easily manipulation to off the mat, in real life and even on the highways.

Most martial arts use sparring to help hone skills like distance, reaction times, where one's weight needs to be, for example. It's not fighting. There are rules, customs, and agreements set up beforehand to minimize injuries and to learn techniques.

For example, you may be learning a new technique to defend yourself from a straightforward punch aimed at your face. The teacher demonstrates the new technique and then you and a partner practice it. Most likely you and your partner would be moving in slow motion to begin with, picking up more speed once you both get the technique perfected more.

This is especially true in Aikido. One of the first few techniques we practice is how to fall to minimize the impact on the body, because most techniques end with the opponent on the mat. Learning to fall safely is going to make practicing more enjoyable.

People who are really stiff and tense make it much easier to apply these martial art techniques or to be able to subdue your opponent.

Another way of looking at this is with *soft* and *pliable* being the opposite of stiff and rigid. For example, if you have ever held a toddler who did not want to be held, you understand this. What do they do? They become super relaxed and noodle-like to try to get away. They slip through your arms. It's *very* difficult to keep holding on to them.

Same with sparring. The stiffer a person is, the easier they are to manipulate. The more relaxed they are (less body tension), the harder it is.

Why do I bring this up in a book about driving with more compassion?

Because ...

In the Real World—Rigid Minds Are Easily Manipulated

Remember that sentence in the yoga book that changed my life—how a flexible body helps to maintain a flexible mind?

Put that in context with a stiff mind, a mind that is inflexible, staunchly opinionated, easily offended, and voila, that mind is easily manipulated.

We may need to keep an open mind to make changes—even driving changes—of our habits. Seeing how we can easily be manipulated by outside influences takes awareness and an open mind. Second, I think the world needs open-mindedness right now. We have mastered the rigid mind. Third, I believe rigid thinking or dogmatism is unhealthy. For individuals, for our communities, and for the Earth.

Here is one definition of dogmatism, from the National Institutes of Health (NIH):

The avoidance from accepting other's beliefs, ideas, and behaviors. Dogmatic individuals have many problems in understanding new ideas. They cannot accept reasonable ideas instead of their (maybe) faulty ideas. They do not cooperate with others with different ideas.

Dogmatism is one of the factors that have a negative effect on wellbeing.

Closed, rigid, dogmatic thinking is the recipe for unhappiness.

Or, as Buddha said, "Those who cling to perceptions and views wander the world offending people." This quote, and many others by Buddha, can be found at www.realbuddhaquotes.com.

Turn Signals and Temper Tantrums: The Saga of the Blinker Vigilante

Here is a perfect example of a rigid mind and someone who can be easily manipulated. I was visiting one of my sisters in North Carolina in 2012. We are driving to Target to get garden supplies and are stopped at a red light, waiting to turn right into the parking lot.

A big Ford truck in front of us had a large handwritten sign on a piece of plywood attached to the back. In huge red letters, it said USE YOUR BLINKERS. This sign took up the whole back of his truck. The skull and crossbones added to its aggressiveness. He clearly was a blinker vigilante.

I agree that using your blinkers helps other drivers to know what you are planning and really helps with safety on the road. But to me, the choice to use your blinkers or not, was a truly small thing to armor up about. I mean, there are so many causes in our world to be an activist about and he picks not using blinkers?

The light turned green, and we started to drive and got ready to turn into the parking lot when this USE-YOUR-BLINKERS truck in front of us stopped at the crosswalk.

He waited till the light changed to yellow, then turned into the parking lot. Now the light was red again, for us, and we couldn't turn. We were stuck waiting through another red light.

Why did he do that?

Until we realized that, oh, my sister didn't have her blinkers on.

I still can't wrap my head around this person's behavior. Talk about rigid and dogmatic thinking. And behaving. He was actually looking into his rearview mirror to see if anyone wasn't using their blinkers behind him in the double-turn lane and then taking revenge by making them sit through another light.

Talk about being so easily manipulated. Want to make this guy mad? Easy-peasy, just don't use your blinkers.

My whole point here is that rigid, dogmatic thinking is going to toss you around like a beach ball in a hurricane. Being so easily triggered and having your "buttons" so effortlessly pushed is, to me, an unhealthy, stressful way to live. Might you have some rigid thinking while driving? I certainly found some ways my thinking was rigid and very judgmental, which I will share more of in the last chapter. It had to do with people who I deemed selfish—therefore, less-than and lower on my what-a-good-human-should-be-like scale—on the road.

A Curious, Open-Minded Texan

I was working with a first-time acupuncture client, who I'll call "Gary," from the local Chamber of Commerce. He had come to the ribbon-cutting ceremony of the new day spa that I owned. He was a very kind and professionally successful person. I rarely saw him not wearing a nice suit and a smile.

He did one acupuncture treatment with me, and I didn't see him again for acupuncture. In fact, I lost contact with him after leaving that Chamber and then eventually closing the day spa.

I ran into him at a coffee shop a few years later. I was chatting with a friend, and he came up and introduced himself to my friend. We hugged, and he sat down with us. He told my friend how we had met and then shared something that blew my mind. He said, "Connie changed my life!"

Wait, what!? Quite frankly, I wondered how little old me had accomplished this.

He then went on to explain.

After the ribbon-cutting ceremony, he decided to make that acupuncture appointment. He said he wanted to get out of the comfort zone of his Texan ideas about alternative medicine being "way out there." He went on to speak a little about the beliefs he grew up with and how he had wanted to try to expand them.

Apparently, that one acupuncture treatment opened and expanded his beliefs and he wanted to know more about alternative medicines. He then tried various energy treatments and thoroughly resonated with essential oils and their benefits. He delved deeper into their values and became quite skilled at using essential oils for optimum health.

He then went on to tell us essential oils actually saved his sister's life. What!?

His sister had been dealing with an illness for some time and kept getting sicker and sicker. At first, she was not interested in what she called "quackery." Yet nothing else was working, and she became afraid of actually dying. He convinced her to at least try some essential oils. This became the turning point for managing her health. For her, using essential oils changed the trajectory of her illness and began her path back to better health.

"All because of you, Connie!"

Wowza, I'd had no idea this had gone on for him. And of course, *I* did not change his beliefs, *he* did!

Gary's journey gave me pause to reflect on how the power of curiosity and open-mindedness set into motion a series of actions that affected not only his life but also others around him. Gary's courage to step outside his comfort zone, to explore and withhold judgment, opened doors to a world of new possibilities. Every step into the unknown, every attitude of curiosity, has the potential to change and transform our lives and all those we are connected to. The wake we leave certainly has a ripple effect.

I believe we live in a web of connection with all others, and we are either adding grace and kindness or the opposite.

Could being open-minded on the road, giving more grace to

people's mistakes, to our mistakes, make our world a better place?

I challenge you, dear reader, to see if you can experience this.

Our Thoughts as Medicine

To conclude this chapter on driving with awareness and compassion to benefit our mental health, I would like to say driving is one area of our lives that we can use to bring awareness to our thoughts, or narrative, about what is happening in the moment and endeavor toward the positive.

This is one way to manage stress and promote well-being and more happiness.

And it's not so much our thoughts as medicine, it's the *awareness* of our thoughts that is powerful medicine. It gives us choices.

Bringing our awareness to our thoughts, with kindness and compassion, is indeed a lifelong journey. It's not easy, but worth the effort. More on how this is done in Part V.

For now, let's get off autopilot and endeavor to catch our thoughts, our stories, and then we can make the *choice* to follow the ones that will grow our soul, and bring compassion to ourselves and our wake.

CHAPTER 5:

Becoming a More Compassionate Driver Is Bigger Than You

*"We are all affecting the world every moment, whether we
mean to or not. Our actions and states of mind matter because
we are so deeply interconnected with one another."*
—Ram Dass

YES, BEING A MORE MINDFUL, kindful, and compassionate
driver is going to help the person behind the wheel—you, dear reader.
It also benefits the imprisoned passengers in your car. I can't tell you
how many people, when I told them what I was writing about, wanted
a copy to give their boyfriend, girlfriend, spouse, and so on. And it
will benefit all those around you. What is the wake we want to leave
behind for others to experience?

Caring about the Wake You Leave Behind

Can we bring our *inner*, natural human goodness to the *outer* experience of driving?

Never again do I want to leave a wake behind me like I did that day when I was driving to go paddleboarding.

I am using the boating term "wake" as a metaphor for the ripple effect our actions have. Like a boat that can leave behind small, gentle waves or harsh, crashing ones, our actions and attitudes can leave gentleness and kindness, or harshness and callousness, behind us.

When I started this journey, I felt if I could be just a little more compassionate while driving, it could easily spill out into more areas of my life. Driving is only one piece of this greater mindfulness journey. It's a great place to practice because it can be exceedingly challenging. We often can't comprehend, at all, why people do the things they do on the road.

Sounds like life to me!

As Ram Dass states, we are all interconnected. If we can become more mindful and kindful and compassionate with ourselves, this energy radiates out into the web of life. We are ultimately always affecting the world. It's just a matter of how we want to do that—in positive, uplifting ways or negative ways.

Instead of speeding to rage, could I speed to compassion?

Like paying for someone's coffee behind you at the drive-thru, letting someone merge into your lane is an act of kindness. It could almost guarantee that you, and the person behind you, will add more kindness toward someone else that day.

I am assuming, if you have read this far, that this—caring about the wake you leave behind—is important to you.

Wave a Gun?

A friend of mine, years ago, told me her brother wanted to put a gun rack in his truck, on the window behind his seat, to hold a rifle. Then he could pick it up and aim it at a driver he felt did something stupid and give them a good scare. That's not the kind of wake I want to leave behind.

I want to share a non-driving experience about how we affect others. It was another humbling experience for me, a reminder of the wake I can leave and what I learned from it.

Life in the Friendly Skies (but Not at the Hotel)

I was a flight attendant in my early twenties, young, carefree, and learning to be social in other cultures with people who didn't grow up in Wisconsin. This began my experience of seeing the cultural differences from state to state. For example, Wisconsinites, i.e., Midwesterners, are very different, in my experience as a flight attendant, from Bostonians, i.e., East Coasters, in general.

Here's a perfect example: I'm on an early morning flight from a Midwestern town, and I'm asking people on board if they want cream or sugar with their coffee. Most of them shyly say something like, "Yes, I would love some cream if it's not too much of a bother."

My experience on another flight later that day to a southern, oceanside town: A passenger's flight-attendant button goes off—twice—about thirty seconds after the wheels come up. I unbuckle my seat belt and walk up the aisle, my body at a forty-five-degree angle. The passenger wants a rum and coke. "No, sir, we cannot serve you (your cocktail) till the plane levels off and we can push the carts up the aisle. Could you please turn off your flight-attendant button, thank you."

Later in my airline career, when I became a concourse agent, I learned that when a New York flight was delayed, they would reach out to an agent who was from New York to announce this delay to the passengers. They found this kept the frustration levels lower than if they were told about the delay from a non-New Yorker's accent.

In this particular story about how we leave a wake, the six-person crew and I had been flying all day. This was day three of our four-day trip, and we were to have a layover in Boston. This was not my favorite hotel, as I heard too many stories about it being haunted. I could totally believe it! By the time we arrived at the hotel, it was late at night, and I felt exhausted. I was looking forward to being horizontal and not moving.

I was the first to get my hotel key and talked with the crew to find out what time we would meet in the morning to catch our shuttle back to the airport. Then I was off to my hotel room. Many times, airline crews are given the furthest rooms from the elevator, and this day was no different.

I took the elevator up to my floor, pulled my luggage for this four-day trip, and walked down one long hallway, turned, walked down another long hallway, turned and you guessed it, my room was the last door down the hallway. So, I was a little peeved.

Finally, I reached the door of my room. I was so looking forward to sleep. I opened the door, but it only opened as far as the chain would allow. Someone was *in* this room! I heard voices and quickly shut the door as quietly as I could. I had heard rumors that this hotel was haunted, but if it was, I felt pretty sure the ghosts wouldn't have put the chain on the door.

Now, I was no longer peeved; I was short of both rage and a meltdown. I pulled my luggage behind me, walked the long halls, took the elevator back to the first floor, and proceeded to the front desk.

When I arrived at the front desk, there was only one young woman behind it, no one else (they were probably sleeping).

She looked up at me with a nice smile and asked how she could help me. I said—maybe with a slight smartass tone—"Could I get a key to a room that doesn't have anyone else in it ... by chance?"

Okay, so maybe I had a full smartass tone.

She then looked about as mortified as I was, eyes wide and a little red in the face. Embarrassed, she quickly moved to the computer to find another room for me, apologizing the whole time.

She stopped typing and provided me with another key. I turned (feeling righteously angry) and went back up the elevator and walked back down what seemed like equally long hallways, reaching my (hopefully not) haunted hotel room.

The next morning, the flight crew and I were on the hotel shuttle to the airport, and I shared my experience with the others. Another flight attendant, Linda (not her real name) said the same thing had happened to her! She had also gone back down to get a different room. She said she and the front desk person had some laughs, understanding that these things happen, and joked about why Bostonians don't pronounce the letter *R*. She got a new room and was off to get some rest.

Shortly after Linda arrived at her new room, the woman at the front desk sent up a bottle of champagne for her with a note thanking her for her understanding.

I'm sure you know the answer to this, but did I get a bottle of champagne sent up to my room?

Nope.

Hmm, I wonder why? Maybe if I had treated the young woman with courtesy, kindness, and respect, I might have had a nice bottle of champagne that would have maybe kept me from sleeping with one eye open looking for ghosts (and maybe I would have learned why

Bostonians don't say their *R*s).

The goal, of course, isn't to expect champagne if you are kind. The exchange of kind, respectful energy is so much more rewarding and humane on its own. I lost out on a feel-good experience with my dehumanizing behavior. I didn't leave an inspiring wake, that is for sure. Neither I nor the receptionist left that situation feeling good.

What goes around, comes around.

The saying that *happy people don't hurt people* was certainly true for me in this instance, just as it was when I was on my way to go paddleboarding at the quarry. And, I do believe what makes us all part of a common humanity is our deep desire to **want to be happy.**

No, we are not happy people all the time, *but* do we need to puke out our unhappiness at others?

What We Do When We Are Inconvenienced

So much of driving frustration comes because we are being inconvenienced.

I have contemplated this issue of being inconvenienced a great deal. I believe it's natural to get frustrated and irritated when we perceive something is going to mess with our plans or maybe even our comfort. Especially if you are already in a stressful situation.

Yet, I still have a choice in how I want to respond.

I love the following story, versions of which are often shared on social media, and how it illustrates what can come out of us:

> You are holding a cup of coffee when someone comes along and bumps into you or shakes your arm, making you spill your coffee everywhere.
> Why did you spill the coffee?

"Because someone bumped into me!"

Wrong answer (possibly).

You spilled the coffee because there was coffee in your cup.

Had there been tea in the cup, you would have spilled tea.

Whatever is inside the cup is what will spill out.

Therefore, when life comes along and shakes you (which WILL happen), whatever is inside you will come out. It's easy to fake it, until you get rattled.

So we have to ask ourselves ... "What's in my cup?"

When life gets tough, what spills over?

Joy, gratefulness, peace, and humility?

Anger, bitterness, harsh words, and reactions?

Life provides the cup, *you* choose how to fill it.

They say the highest form of love is grace. Can I cultivate grace more; fill my cup up with more grace and less self-righteousness and needing to control?

Could I become that driver who gives grace to all other drivers—including myself?

I certainly am trying!

Tension's Ripple Effect on the Soul

Can we be working on our souls while working on not being angry drivers?

I believe we can.

I joined a spiritual group in my late twenties to understand more about my soul or my true nature. It was run by Carolyn Young, M.Div., and the workshop was called "A Woman's Journey Home." Ms. Young is a forty-year student of the Diamond Approach, which centers on the practice of self-inquiry in the investigation of the self and one's experience.

"A Woman's Journey Home" was meant to be a three-week course, but it went so well it ended up being a three-decade journey.

Through the three decades of my work with what we eventually named the "Luminous Ladies" group, we mainly worked on our soul and our psychology (mind and body) through understanding our body tensions. During this journey, Ms. Young gave us all a book written by a dear friend of hers, Rhea Powers, having mostly to do with dealing with our inner critic or superego.

Remember back when I was driving to the quarry to go paddleboarding, and after the embarrassingly unkind incident, when I was attempting to not beat myself up? Well, it was because of the work on dealing with my inner critic with the Luminous Ladies that came to my rescue.

I want to share a passage from this book because it was and is another reason for my "why" in my driving journey. In *Unfolding the Soul*, Rhea Powers says, "A tense body equals a tense soul."

Relaxation in the soul creates relaxation in the body. Likewise, relaxation in the body can contribute to relaxation in the soul. It is possible to work on the soul by working on the body. Working on the soul can produce a change in the body. Simply bringing awareness to the tension in the body can help relax the soul.

I believe strongly, as Powers says, that a consistently tense body equals a tense soul. If this doesn't resonate with you, dear reader, I ask that you bring some curiosity and sense into your tensions and feel what comes up.

Certainly, one of my biggest "whys" in this journey of becoming a more compassionate driver was this spiritual piece of, once again, cultivating more and more of the good or more skillful, wolf traits.

One of my acupuncture clients, who I treat for various types of chronic pain in her body (due to a car accident, part of her spine is fused), had gone on a two-week cruise. She told me that for those two weeks, she had none of the chronic pain or the occasional digestive issues. She wasn't at her (stressful) desk job and I'm sure a heck of a lot more relaxed, joyful, and happy. Did this relaxed vacation bring out her true nature, her more soulful qualities—thus allowing more freedom from pain? Interesting question to stay curious about.

For me, personally, the less tension I have in my body, in the stories I'm rolling around in my head, the more in touch I am with the part of my good or skillful wolf. Driving around constantly tense was not going to make my soul happy.

Emotional Bypassing—Navigating Traffic, Navigating Emotions

Emotional bypassing, sometimes called spiritual bypassing, takes place when we avoid fully acknowledging or experiencing our emotions. This tendency occurs when we deem certain emotions as negative, not socially enjoyed, or accepted. And here's the big one: these feelings are deemed not spiritual. It's not spiritual to feel envy, revenge, hatred, so we pretend, thus repressing, that we don't actually feel these human emotions. It's simply a spiritual façade.

My biggest hurdle in the early stages of my journey of becoming a more mindful, kindful driver was navigating and processing my anger and frustration—the less pleasant aspects of the driving experience (truly an understatement, wouldn't you say).

Confronting the discomfort was a major challenge for me, and I have to admit I can be quite good at emotional or spiritual bypassing. If bypassing were an Olympic sport, I could become a gold medalist.

I went to pick up my daughter from the Denver airport one late afternoon as she returned from a long international trip.

I would be taking several packed highways that would be even more overcrowded at rush hour. I am the queen of side roads, to infuse my driving with some sense of peace and relaxation, but this was not going to be one of those trips.

The journey involved navigating highways that were what I call "parking lots" because we were hardly moving. It involved being assertive and hypervigilant to aggressive maneuvers, constant lane changes, and gridlock. On *every* highway, including the exit and entrance ramps.

I was trying to remain an unflappable adult. I couldn't tell if driving in a snowstorm would be worse or not.

I made it onto I-70 and guess what? It was another parking lot! I kept trying like the dickens to keep my body and mind calm and relaxed, all the while, I needed to be "on" and "aggressive."

Stuff the "aggressiveness"—that's not lady-like.

I got off I-70 to get onto Peña Boulevard, and for the first time in thirty-three years of going to the airport, the boulevard was a parking lot. Bumper-to-bumper cars. Once again, it took close to fifteen minutes to get off the entrance ramp alone!! Ahhhh, I wanted to scream! I mean, genuinely scream at the thorough ineptness of our road system.

But no, I just stuffed it down so I could be civil. Be a "nice, kind" person.

I was most certainly going to be late to pick up my daughter. One more little push into the sympathetic (flight, fright) nervous system.

Finally, I arrived at the airport to pick up my daughter, who was just fine waiting for me to get there.

The trip back was slightly better, but not by much. We reached our house, and a box was sitting by our door. It was the Christmas gift I'd bought for my husband. I was happy I could quickly hide it before he was able to see the label on the box and figure out what the gift was.

My daughter and I were then going to watch a Netflix show we were binging. We went downstairs to the family room. I was going to hide the Christmas present in the family room closet.

I had a difficult time getting the box into the closet. I had to squeeze and angle my body between our granddaughter's kitchen set and a very long piece of elliptical exercise equipment. My body was torqued as I continued to push the box onto one of the shelves, and then ... I lost it. I got angry at the box and started swearing loudly.

I finally took a breath and looked at my daughter, whom I had just made very uncomfortable (rightly so). She was trying to say things to soothe me, make things right, calm.

I simply told her, "I am responsible for my behavior." I'd just spent three hours trying to remain calm and peaceful, attempting to be an unflappable adult. I had been minimizing and bypassing my frustration and anger. These buried emotions finally found an outlet in the challenge of hiding a simple Christmas gift.

Learning to not spiritually bypass was very big on the journey. In Part III, I talk a lot about how to overcome this.

How I Would Make That Drive Today

In theory, here is what I would do differently.

First, I would call my daughter to let her know I was going to be late so she could take care of herself in whatever way that meant. So much of my frustration was thinking I was letting my daughter down by being late. She was just fine waiting and reading a delicious novel that she was devouring with intensity.

Second, I would have found a fun and uplifting podcast to feel good about all the time spent on the road.

Third, I would check in with my body to see if there was tension building up. For me, anger and frustration can be found in my solar plexus (the area below one's sternum) and in the tightening of my jaw. Sometimes I can relax the tension, and other times, it is the awareness of the tension that is helpful.

Fourth, I would have taken up my daughter's request to drive us home. (Again, trying to be that unflappable adult).

Another thing I may do, because I would be by myself, would be to make up a nonsensical song labeling my emotions. This is a way to not bypass my emotions and get a little chuckle for the stupidity of the song. It could go something like this:

Did I tell you how much I hate I-25, hate I-25, hate I-25!?
Oh look, there is another driver who thinks they are the only ones on the road, road, road.
What a toad, what a toad, what a toad.

Driving is often an utterly stressful experience. Give yourself grace by owning the emotions that come up and have some go-to's that you figure out work for you. I have more of my go-to's, techniques that work for me to help with the stress of driving in Part V.

Accelerating (or Decelerating) Compassion

As I have mentioned throughout this book, and will again, the web of life we weave, the wake we leave, and what we send downriver, are all crucially important. Being compassionate and caring about what wake I leave is all about spirituality. To oversimplify, spirituality is about Love, with a capital "L." There has been too much time spent driving where that—compassion, love—was not coming out of me.

I will finish this section with the powerful words of Nick Cave about how all of our actions are important.

Remember that ultimately we make things happen through our actions, way beyond our understanding or intentions; that our seemingly small ordinary human acts have untold consequences; that what we do in this world means something .... Our deeds, no matter how insignificant they may feel, are replete with meaning and of vast consequence, and that they constantly impact upon the unfolding story of the world, whether we know it or not.

This line of his has been especially powerful for me:

"The everyday human gesture is always a heartbeat away from the miraculous."

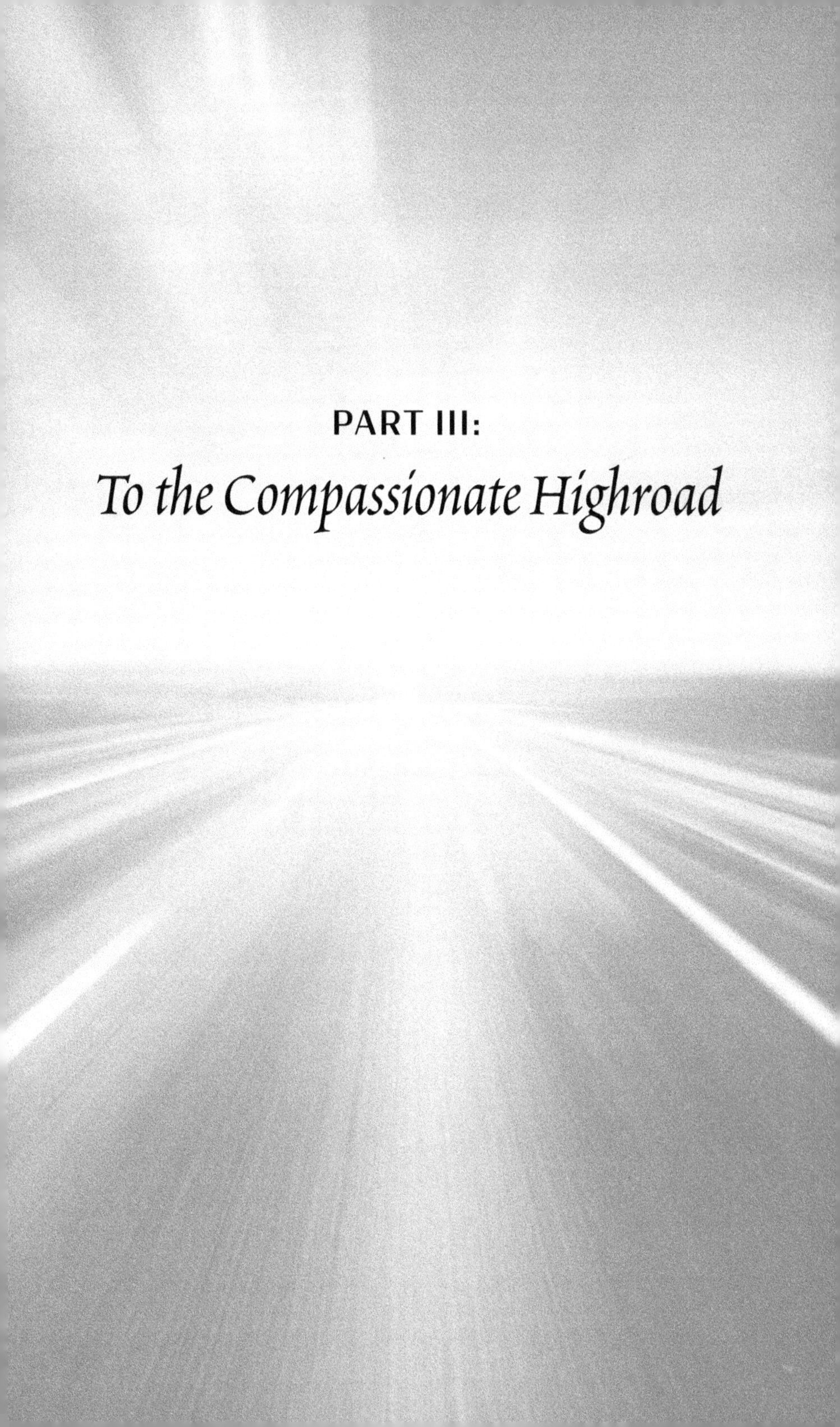

PART III:

To the Compassionate Highroad

CHAPTER 6:

Step One: Observe Yourself—Compassionately

*"Our own worst enemy could never harm us as
much as our own unwise thoughts."*
—The Buddha

IN EVERY SITUATION, as I'm sure you know (never hurts to be reminded as repetition is key to learning), there are so many ways one can respond. You can probably think back to certain moments in your life and wish you had responded differently. We all can—this is a universal human experience.

We give our power away when we let others dictate our reactions. Giving away our power means that we don't think we have any influence over our choices. Someone does *this* and we have to respond like *that*. We don't take responsibility for our actions. Like the Blinker Guy who's driving himself crazy because of others' behaviors. He's making himself extremely unhappy and throwing his power away, all because some people are not using their blinkers.

If you want, dear reader, make a declaration today that you have a desire to keep your power, you want to make healthy choices, and want to be part of the Mindful, Kindful, Compassionate Drivers Club.

Here are the steps I took:

Firstly: Begin to observe my negative responses while driving—with compassion.

Secondly: Note the stories I make up.

Thirdly: Change the stories to something positive.

Lastly: Endeavor to not have any stories.

I came up with these steps using the principles from all of my practices (yoga, meditation, martial arts) that through mindfulness, we encourage harmony of body, mind, and spirit. Disharmony between these is not helpful for health and vitality—which are imperative to being a happy human.

These practices were helping in many areas of my life, and now I wanted them to help me on this journey to be a more mindful, kindful, compassionate driver.

When 70 Percent Isn't a Passing Grade

The first step, knowing where you are starting from, is an important step in any journey, especially when we endeavor to expand our capacities. Which is what this journey is all about—expanding our capacity to have more compassion and less hardness toward our fellow human beings and to our own precious self.

A few years ago, one of my sisters told me she was trying not to swear anymore. I didn't think she swore a lot, to begin with, but it made me think about how often *I* swear. I didn't think I did a lot of swearing, but upon making a conscious effort to bring awareness to my swearing, I have to say I could be quite the old sailor sometimes. That doesn't even count for the swearing in my head.

Like observing my swearing, I began the endeavor of observing myself and my thoughts, while driving. How often was I really pouring toxins into my body with my not-positive thoughts?

How often was I judge-y, irritated, frustrated, swearing, when I was driving? How often was I caught up in not-nice, mean-spirited, made-up stories about drivers? As it turns out, like my swearing, it was way more than I thought. I must admit, it was almost seven out of ten times I drove. Yuck!

I came up with that 70 percent by deciding, after each trip, how often my thoughts regarding driving were ugly.

Some examples of my self-talk:

"What the hell, you have a jeep and you slow down for that dip? You cannot even call yourself a 'jeep' driver!"

"OMG, what color green do you need to press the gas pedal?!"

*"You could have just put on your blinker! You're not the only one on the road—***hole. I would have gone around you had you let me know!"*

Really!? I'm more Genghis Khan than Gandhi! While driving, at least. Again, this was a bit hard to take in.

Ahhh, it's never easy seeing the ugly side of yourself, is it?

If you do an internet search on how many hours we spend driving you will find results for anywhere between fifteen to twenty-five hours *per* month.

That is a lot of time to be making oneself unhappy and unhealthy, and remember, you carry over that unhappiness after you are done driving. It doesn't magically disappear when you turn the car off.

Personally, I would love to transform that negativity time into a more life-enhancing time. More positive vibes and good-chemical releasing time for my body and mind.

Before approaching Step One of observing our negative reactions, I want to bring up four essential elements to help with this endeavor: self-compassion and the Inner Critic, and mindfulness versus mindlessness.

The Necessity of Bringing in Kindness and Compassion

I *had* to bring in that kindness, that self-compassionate piece. Like I did on the way to the quarry to go paddleboarding, or when I heard myself wanting others to take care of themselves, so I didn't have to wait to make my turn. Otherwise, it's extremely difficult (almost impossible) to look at and *see* the nasty or ugly parts of ourselves. And it's not about being "perfect."

No one is perfect. Let's just drop the perfectionist goals from our lives. In case you need some validation or inspiration to not strive for perfection, here is what Brené Brown has to say. This is from her book *The Gifts of Imperfection*:

Understanding the difference between healthy striving and perfectionism is critical to laying down the shield and picking up your life. Research shows that perfectionism hampers success. In fact, it's often the path to depression, anxiety, addiction, and life paralysis.

Over three years of endeavoring to be a mindful, kindful driver and ... well, I still have my moments. I'd say my negative self-talk while driving is closer to 20 percent of the time, and always depends on my life-force energy. I notice that when I'm content, easeful, and happy, it's a good day. Stressed, tired, and hungry, maybe not a good day.

This *is* the challenge!

Sometimes, even with the best of intentions, we don't stay on that soul quality side, or the Zen Calm side of the Yes/And Table in Part I. There are times we are just human and, for example, become mean, judgmental, and even use our power destructively.

I have made up a word that helps with that cognitive dissonance. Remember, this is the concept about the tension caused in our psyche/body when our behavior doesn't match how we really want to be. It can be exceedingly hard to look at our flaws or shortcomings.

I call it my *cute-ugly*. It's the inner critic I've mentioned a few times. Everyone has one, it's just a matter of the degree you listen to it and believe it.

"Oh, how cute, that ugly is coming up again."

It's about not shaming myself. I wanted a way to look at my shortcomings without going into shame.

I can't tell you how hard it was to not beat myself up—to let my inner critic win the gold medal that day—for raging at that young driver.

Now, when I see a cute-ugly, my internal dialogue may look like this:

"Look at the cute-ugly impatience, making you blame, blame, blame."

"OMG, look at how judgmental I'm being! Good catch ... let it go!"

"That was so hard-hearted, Connie. What's going on underneath this hard heart of yours?"

It can be hard to accept all the ugly conversations going on in your head when you become aware of them. **The opposite of self-criticism and the inner critic is self-compassion.**

Shifting Gears from Inner Critic Voice to Self-Compassion Voice

Remember when I mentioned the superego? Also known as the Judge or the Judge Within, or the Inner Critic? Where Rhea Powers wrote a whole book on recognizing and not succumbing to this critical voice?

Becoming more aware of that critical voice so that you can switch it to something more compassionate is essential to being a kinder driver and a kinder person.

The aggression and judgment we direct outward—say, to the drivers around us—is a direct reflection of the aggression and judgment we are allowing in our inner world. We are simply providing ourselves with a break by directing this judgment outward.

Another way to say this is that if we are not busy judging and criticizing others, those judgments and criticisms are waiting for *us*.

When we allow this critical inner voice to take over—whether it is directed inward, at ourselves, or outward, at that lady who just took forever to park—we are diverting our own life-force energy to a voice that criticizes endlessly, who cannot be pleased, who makes everything ugly and mean and small.

Is that what *you* want? Is that what *I* wanted?

I don't think so.

Remember the zen calm I talked about? That's what I want. And I'll bet you want it, too.

So, endeavor to chill out. Pay attention when that superego starts in on you or that lady or your mom or your kid or whoever. Divert. Peace out.

"How do I do that?" you ask ...

First, recognize it. Recognize when the superego gets started. The mindfulness practices in the Appendix will be extremely effective for this.

Second, acknowledge it. Is this helpful or useful for me right now? Now you have the choice to think, say, do, feel something else. I attempted to do this, with some success, on the drive to the quarry.

This is medicine. It is medicine for you, for me, and for the world.

Any one of us can judge another. Not a problem. *Opting out of* the judgment the moment we sense it is what matters.

That's the medicine.

This is how my journey began.

And this is how yours can begin, too.

Discovering Self-Compassion

Did you grow up in a household that taught about compassion? About self-compassion? How to treat yourself with kindness and love? Were you taught about the inner critic inside your head? If you made a mistake, you were told to say you were sorry, and also be compassionate and kind to that human side of you? If you did, you are in a rare minority group.

Were you taught to be tender toward yourself?

Not to fault anyone, because most people are doing their best, but did you grow up to where somehow you found yourself an Olympic Champion at self-criticism? (Another Olympic sport I try not to train for anymore.) A deep sense of feeling unworthy? A deep sense of not being enough?

I know I did.

While on this journey of being a more mindful, compassionate driver, a lot of self-criticisms came up regarding how mean and nasty my thoughts could be.

I read an extremely helpful article on self-compassion that I want to share parts of here. In an interview in *Greater Good* magazine, Kristin Neff, author of *Self-Compassion; The Proven Power of Being Kind to Yourself,* stated that three things are needed for self-compassion to happen:

Self-kindness
Common humanity
Mindfulness

Let's look at what Kristin Neff means by these three things that can help us with having more compassion toward ourselves.

Self-Kindness, Common Humanity, and Mindfulness

"First, it requires self-kindness, that we be gentle and understanding with ourselves rather than harshly critical and judgmental."

Yes, let's add this to our journey of becoming a more mindful, kindful, compassionate driver. Kindness toward ourselves, that same kindness we give others but forget to give ourselves.

"Second, it requires recognition of our common humanity, feeling connected with others in the experience of life rather than feeling isolated and alienated by our suffering."

Feeling connected to others rather than feeling isolated is the opposite of what happens when we are driving. As mentioned before, we are anonymous in our steel cage. Much like we see in social media comments that get really heated because we can remain isolated. This all leads to a lot of dehumanizing of others and not having to be responsible for the mean wake we leave.

This concept of our common humanity is enormously important to understand for our driving. And wouldn't it be so sweet if we left that wake not only while driving but in our whole lives.

Ms. Neff's third piece of action needed to experience self-compassion:

"Third, it requires mindfulness—that we hold our experience in balanced awareness, rather than ignoring our pain or exaggerating it. We must achieve and combine these three essential elements in order to be truly self-compassionate."

I love the use of her words "balanced awareness." Not ignoring, stuffing, or bypassing on one end of the emotional spectrum and also not exaggerating emotions, like that beachball in a hurricane.

The term *balanced awareness* is used in many definitions of mindfulness (below are a few), sometimes phrased as "awareness without judgment."

It's hard to look at our cute-ugly.

It is hard to see our own impatience, greed, jealousy, and rage. One of the ways I have found was a form of grace. Like when we look at a small child having an absolute temper tantrum, and we think, *How cute, you get that rage out at not having another cookie.* The temper tantrum is cute because they're *kids*!

(If you are still having temper tantrums at being denied another cookie, there are, most likely, other books you should be reading.)

Now as an adult, when we throw a tantrum, most likely only in our heads, it's not cute. It's rather ugly. But let's give ourselves a break. Life in a human body is hard.

It's this type of grace I'm endeavoring for myself and my humanness. It's the type of grace you can endeavor to reach for yourself and *your* humanness.

For example, I may start to feel like a victim, thinking, *Oh, poor me*, when stuck on I-70 trying to get to the mountains and the highway is wall-to-wall stopped cars. No one is moving and people are running to the side of the road, sneaking away to relieve themselves. This is the worst thing ever. Poor me!

If I'm lucky to catch this line of thinking I may say to myself, "Oh, look at that cute-ugly being a victim again. Hmm, what could change this mindset? How can I use this medicine to learn something from?"

Once again, the important part is catching the thoughts. We are still on Part One of becoming the compassionate people we are. Mindfulness practices certainly help. But first, let's look at the opposite of mindfulness.

Mindlessness—Living Unconsciously

Occasionally, getting clarity about something necessitates recognizing what it is *not*.

Is mindlessness the opposite of mindfulness? Are we either mindful or mindless? Hmmm.

I truly believe that if we are not aware and present, mindful, then we are mindless.

Let's look at some definitions of mindlessness.

Merriam-Webster

1. a: marked by a lack of mind or consciousness
b; (1) marked by or displaying no use of the powers of the intellect
(2) requiring little attention or thought
2. not mindful : Heedless

Dictionary.com

1. without intelligence; senseless
2. unmindful or heedless

Connie-ism

1. Being on autopilot

Can you relate to any of these definitions? They give me the yikes. Like driving somewhere and I don't even remember how I got there—so lost in thought.

And "without intelligence?!" Double yikes!

How do we become present, present to the moment with awareness, with intelligence and with our senses?

Waking Up from Autopilot

How do you observe your thoughts if 95 percent of the time we navigate through life on autopilot? Ahhh, the crux of our mental tendencies. The helpful tendencies, and the not-helpful tendencies.

Here's a personal example of waking up from autopilot. One day as I was rolling out my yoga mat, I suddenly became aware of this yucky conversation between my husband and me in my head. It was full of me judging and blaming. From over two years ago! Something that we even had worked through.

With that present-moment awareness (of the very old narrative), I then totally dropped the narrative.

Silence.

Nothing, just stillness.

I just breathed in and out—observing this silence.

I didn't move, I just observed this peace.

I *was* peace.

My next thought was, *This is what the yogis and mystics are saying about liberation, about freedom!*

I recognized the story, decided to drop it, and there it was. Peace!

I didn't need to be caught up in a very old, ugly narrative. I could be free of it if I chose to be.

This is what it can feel like when we wake up and become aware of the cute-ugly. Aware but not engaging with anger, judgment, rage, and self-criticism that often operates in the background.

These moments of awareness are a chance to work on self-compassion.

Let's get back to this mindfulness stuff to understand how we then can have the choice to go off autopilot with compassion.

So, What Is Mindfulness?

I'd like to share a variety of definitions of mindfulness that I think are helpful.

Mindfulness is a state of active, open, attention on the present moment. When you're mindful, you observe your thoughts and feelings from a distance, without judging them good or bad. Instead of letting your life pass you by, mindfulness means living in the moment and awakening to experience.
—*Psychology Today*

Deliberately being present on purpose.
—Said by many

The practice of mindfulness is a gateway into the experience of interconnectedness and interdependence, out of which stem emotionally intelligent action, new ways of being, and ultimately greater happiness, clarity, wisdom and kindness— at work and in the world.
—Jon Kabat-Zinn, foreword to *Search Inside Yourself* by Chade-Meng Tan

Sustained present-moment awareness that itself is neutral with regard to what it is aware of.
—Rick Hanson, *Buddha's Brain: The Practical Neuroscience of Happiness, Love, and Wisdom*

Mindfulness is the gentle effort to be continuously present with experience.
—Bodhipaksa

Life is a dance. Mindfulness is witnessing that dance.
—Amit Ray, PhD, *Mindfulness: Living in the Moment, Living in the Breath*

Noticing what you are experiencing with kindness and curiosity *is* mindfulness.
—Amy Saltzman, MD, *A Still Quiet Place for Athletes*

Mindfulness is a simple practice, but not an easy one ... but you are worth doing hard things.
—Nicole Davis

Practicing Mindfulness

Simple, but not easy. Have you heard this phrase? I hear it all the time when it comes to mindfulness practices, and I kind of hate it. Yet I have to agree here. At the end of the book, in the Appendix, I have some more information about formal and informal mindfulness practices.

For now, let's make it super simple.

Sensing In

A simple way to bring mindfulness or present-moment awareness is to become aware of a sensation.

Go ahead and give yourself one minute to do this mindfulness practice. Read each sentence, then sense your body, before going to the next sentence.

> Become aware of your sit bones if you are sitting. Become aware of your neck and face—release any tension that may be there.
>
> Become aware of any sounds around you.
>
> Become aware of a long, slow in-breath ... then a long, slow, relaxing out-breath.
>
> Notice the belly expanding on the inhale.
>
> Notice the belly contracting on the exhale.
>
> Do two more breaths, long, slow, and deep on the inhale.
>
> Let it feel joyful.
>
> Let the long, slow exhale feel like you are fully letting go and releasing.

How was that?

If you are aware of a sensation in your body, you are on your way to present-moment awareness.

Why?

Because sensations in your body are happening in the present. Unlike being lost in thought, where you can easily be in the future, thinking about what the meeting is going to be like. Or in the past, thinking about a frustrating (or wonderful) conversation you had.

If you are aware of the birds singing, you are present.

If you are aware of bacon cooking, you are present.

If you are aware of your hands on the steering wheel, you are present.

If you are aware of your long, deep in-breath, you are present.

If you are aware of your slow, softening exhale, you are present.

To re-quote Hudson and Riso, "If we are aware of the sensations of our bodies, it is a solid piece of evidence that we are present." The really cool thing is, we have our bodies with us all the time.

The second part to this present-moment awareness is to add that compassionate piece. We are attempting to have compassionate present-moment awareness.

Step One of becoming a more mindful, compassionate driver is to begin to observe our thoughts and stories going on while we are driving. Now we're going on to Step Two and catching our stories and how they add tension to our bodies.

CHAPTER 7:

Step Two: Noticing the Stories and Tensions

"In the absence of enough data, we will always make up stories."
—Brené Brown

BY THIS CHAPTER, you may have figured out how much time you actually spend in the car complaining and having conversations that put toxins in your body-mind. Maybe not, but let's talk about those stories and narratives going on out loud or in our heads.

Let me finish that quote by Brené Brown: "In fact, the need to make up a story, especially when we are hurt, is a part of our most primitive survival wiring."

We most often don't have enough information about other drivers to know what their story is. I think you will be amazed at how creative you are when making up these stories on the road.

Let's bring some awareness to the actual stories and see if there is a pattern and where the tension may be showing up in your body.

Here are some of my experiences and stories with mindfulness—and mindlessness—on my journey.

Why Did the Geese Cross the Road?

This story happened about a year into my driving with compassion journey. I was trying to get out of the busy Costco parking lot. And desperately trying *not* to make up a story.

I don't know about you, but I try to park as far away as possible in those busy parking lots with lots of cars and people. I finished shopping, was attempting to leave the parking lot and just needed to go about 500 feet, then I would be on the street and free of the anxiety-producing parking chaos. Then the car in front of me slowly came to a stop. For no reason at all that I could see. We still had 200 feet before the road out of the parking lot!

To the left of the car in front of me was a lady holding back two golden retrievers pulling on their leashes to walk or run across the parking lot. The dogs clearly saw something that they wanted—across the lot—in front of the car in front of me. Clearly, the dog lady didn't want them to go there. She kept pulling the golden retrievers back to the curb.

I was trying to "keep my seat." I was going to my breath and trying not to make up a story because I realized I didn't know what was going on. Why was the car in front of me stopped? Should I do a light tap on my horn? Was she on her phone? I didn't have any idea, in truth, and I was really trying to stay calm but not doing my best because I was also observing the somewhat subtle tension happening in my body.

Deep breath!

OH! Now I see the reason for the stop. Two huge geese walk past, to the right of the car in front of me. The driver in front of me couldn't drive forward because of these geese.

Deep breath in, wonderful softening exhale. I had the answer for this non-moving car in front of me, and we could continue on. Best of all, I wasn't the honking jerk.

Running a Red Light in a Snowstorm

I love kickboxing as part of my self-care, especially when we wrap up class, and get to do free-form sparring. Pull out all the punches (pun intended).

One day I'm finishing the class with some really powerful punches, hooks, and uppercuts, and I say out loud, "I (punch), hate, (punch), people (punch), who run (punch) red lights." (Three punches.)

This started some talk among the other kickboxing students about their own experiences with people running red lights. One student yelled from across the room, "Just yesterday, I saw an accident because someone ran a red light."

Right!? I felt so justified in this anger.

I continued to HONK LIKE MAD at those cars that ran red lights. *These people are arrogant and selfish. Like they are the only ones on the road that are important.* Opinion much?

Even though I could feel the tension in my body-mind. Thinking (or saying) nasty mean things, increasing my heart rate and body tension, I felt so *right* and justified. These red-light-runners are selfish ***holes that only care about themselves.

That is until one of them ... was me. Yep, I joined the "I'm a selfish ***hole running red lights" club.

I was driving home from work in blizzard-like conditions. Large snowflakes were coming down heavy. It was dusk, which made it that much harder to see, especially with the side-blowing snow. The windshield wipers could barely keep the snow off the windows.

I was the second car in the left-turn lane. The traffic light screwed up, leaving us without an arrow. When I realized this and all the people backed up in the turn lane behind me, I made the decision to follow the car in front of me after the yellow light, and we both ran a red light.

Several cars beeped at me because now they couldn't go on green. And we were in a blizzard, not the best time to be a jerk.

Yes, I was that jerk, and I immediately said to myself, *Remember this ... you don't know their story—give up this animosity.*

Can I give up this story about red-light runners now? The answer to that is yes, I did stop honking at people who ran red lights.

But, before I completely gave that up, I did try to honk at those red-light runners without leaving me with my heart racing. I'm going to tell you, it did not work. At all. My heart would race even if I tried not to have a narrative going on in my head. Honking, the sound of the honk, is simply an activator of the nervous system. Next time you honk, even if it's for a good reason, check in to see if you have increased your heart rate.

Leaving Estes Park with High Expectations

I was leaving after a few wonderful days in retreat right outside of the town of Estes Park, Colorado. I was feeling so grateful to be in the presence of one of my favorite authors, Mark Nepo. The two-day workshop he put on regarding compassion and our souls was full of beautifully thought-provoking material. This was mixed with yoga, good food, and conversations with people all over the world. (Friendly piece of advice: don't assume you know the difference between an Australian accent and a New Zealand accent).

Packing my luggage in the trunk of my car, I felt the sun on my back, smelled the earthy pine trees, and wondered how long this feeling would last. I knew from the many retreats that I've been on that "re-entry" into the real world would best be accomplished with a great deal of awareness.

I felt in harmony with my soul and with all human beings.

Until ...

About ten minutes later, as I drove through the town of Estes Park, and began to merge onto the street, taking us through the quaint town center.

A red and white convertible cut me off!

WTF, really!? You're a lowlife and you're stupid enough to smoke and I'm sure you're a redneck and totally blissfully ignorant that you just cut me off, you jackass.

There you go! Lost that good harmony vibe with myself and the universe in record time. And what a story I was telling myself.

Creative Stories Living Rent-Free in My Head

At one point in my journey to be a more mindful, kindful driver I thought of a quote from Mark Twain, "My life was filled with terrible misfortune, most of which never happened."

The stories I was making up about drivers, thinking back, were darn creative. But stories they were. Most of the drivers I had conversations about in my head were certainly afflicted with terrible misfortune—according to me. And all of it was only in *my* head. Really, all of it was in my body-mind.

"You're too old or young to be on the road."

Story—opinion. I don't have enough information about a driver to know the truth.

"You're the most selfish, arrogant, piece of s*% of a person on this Earth!"

Story—I certainly don't *know* this driver to be so opinionated.

"I don't care if you lost your will to live—just DRIVE!"

My daughter may, or may not, have said that last quote about the person in the car beside us. She had been driving super slow in front of us until she moved into the turn lane. We both cracked up so hard. What a mean thing to say and yet it was so funny. Still—a story. Just because the driver did indeed look like that remark, we didn't have enough information to know how she was feeling.

These stories, these conversations we are having in our heads or out loud are simply dumping toxins—the stress neurotransmitters, cortisol and adrenaline—in our bodies and building bigger neurological grooves in our brains for complaining. We are all on this big ball called Earth to try to lead happy, joyful, meaningful lives. Complaining and making up negative stories is truly counterproductive to a happy life and to any ease while driving!

As the adage goes, stop letting people and made-up stories live rent-free in your head—for your own health and happiness.

CHAPTER 8:

Steps Three and Four: Changing and then Dropping the Stories

"Goodbye Toxins, Hello Healthy."
—Connie

BY THIS CHAPTER, you have an understanding of the stories you creatively make up in your head, so let's have some fun and start to change them so our bodies are not filled with toxins and tensions, zapping our energy and leaving a wake of negativity.

Step 3: Changing the Stories

They are stories you made up, anyway. Why not make up stories that bring peace to your body-mind, keeping your life-force energy flowing with vitality?

We can stop squeezing the cactus.

Here are some of the changes I will make while driving. Feel free to fill in any of your favorites. I hope that you can sense, in your body, the difference between the two sides. And I hope this will give you more motivation to drive to the highroad.

Creative Storytelling Chart

What I've Said	What I May Say Instead
Oh my God, could you turn any slower!	I hope your plants continue to be safe. (Because I turn really slow when I'm bringing my plants home to put in the garden. When do *you* turn a corner super slow?)
You're not even driving the speed limit!	Guess the Universe wants me to slow down. Guess it's time to take three deep breaths and calm the fork down.
You f%*ing idiot, you turned your car in the middle of the fricken road!	Wow, look at that move! I wonder if they received news of their child going to the emergency room right now.
Get off the damn road to figure out where you need to go.	Sending you lots of good energy. I know what it's like to be lost, not knowing which way to go.
Get off the bleeping phone.	I've been there, done that. I really hope you don't hurt yourself or anyone else because of that choice.
Hello! It's green. Do you need a particular shade of green?	Is the universe asking me to slow down? To pause?
Doesn't anyone have a sense of urgency today?	Same as above.

My hope, dear reader, is you can feel the difference between the left and right side of the chart in your body. Then, take this into the real world of driving, and have fun making up stories that are funny or simply more relaxing.

One of the things I also began to notice with this practice was when people were being genuinely nice, letting people in their lane, slowing down, and hand gesturing to let pedestrians pass. I became more aware of positive actions, not just the negative ones.

Again, have fun and be creative in a positive way.

Step Four: Dropping the Stories

For me, this was and continues to be the hardest step. Yet it is genuinely worth it! A still, quiet mind is a beautiful thing. If you can accomplish this on the road, think how it could affect your life. I will be talking more about the beauty of a quiet mind in Part IV. But for now, if you would like to experience a still, quiet mind, do this. Take a long, slow, deep breath in and suspend your breath. Keep your shoulders relaxed. Maybe even for three seconds, and notice the suspended stillness. Then, slowly exhale. Fully. And again, suspend the exhale and notice the stillness.

How does your body feel?

How do you drop a story? Like you would drop a hot coal. As soon as you become aware—*ding*—you let the story go, let it die. Let there be seconds of stillness.

I do have to admit that this is way easier on days that are going smoothly. I've slept well, ate well, the day outside is my perfect temperature, my relationships are great, everything is well with the world. So much easier to simply let go of that which doesn't serve my well-being. But alas, not every day is like this. Yes, more and more as

I keep my practices up and my practice of being kind on the road is helping me have more of those peaceful days. Yet, life happens.

A Highroad Win for Connie

I'm stopped at a red light, and the car in front of me has a large bumper sticker making fun of a political party. I have a hard time when any political side (or anyone) resorts to dehumanizing people. Yet ...

I sat there and read it a few times, and .... Nothing.

I didn't even go into a silent rant or story in my head. I didn't have to drop the story because I didn't even make one up.

I was amazed at myself! Not in a superiority type of way; just a feel-good win for all the effort I had been putting into dropping the stories. Most of the time these wins happen when all the criteria above have been met. But that's okay. It's beautiful when it happens.

I can't tell you how wonderfully peaceful and content I can feel when I recognize I didn't go into story mode. And that is my hope for you, dear reader!

I love this next parable as it really drives (ha) the message home about what I am talking about.

Two Monks

You might have heard this story about the two monks. Though the author is unknown, it has been repeated many times.

Two monks were walking back to their temple after doing some errands. It had rained a great deal earlier and there were a lot of large puddles on the dirt roads.

As they were about to cross a street, they noticed a young lady with bags hanging from her arms, trying to walk around all the puddles. She was having a difficult time, especially because she had on a long skirt with good shoes.

One of the monks asked if she would like some help, and she was so thankful.

All he could do was pick her up and let her down after a big puddle.

Again, she shared her thanks for not having to muddy her skirt and shoes.

The remainder of their journey back to the temple took about two more hours. Just as they were about to go through the gate, the second monk spoke to the one who had helped the lady and said, "I can't believe you touched that lady. We are not supposed to do that."

The first monk replied, "I put that lady down two hours ago. Why are you still carrying her?"

Just drop it.
Let it go.
Or be willing to *try* and let a story go. And stay with that experience.

A Practice of Remembering and Forgetting

Recognizing, becoming aware of our stories, gives us the consciousness to make a choice and get off autopilot. It's a powerful practice!

And as with most practices, there needs to be consistency, and the
exercise really is never ending. This is a lifelong practice. We remember
our heartful self, our good wolf, and then life happens and we harden,
and the not-good wolf comes out. Let self-compassion arise each time.

You won't magically never harden again. But the good news is, we
can become more mindful and compassionate at any moment, too.

PART IV:

The Medicine in the
Highroad Journey

CHAPTER 9:

Our Relationship to Red Lights

*"Incredible change happens in your life when you
decide to take control of what you do have power over
instead of craving control over what you don't."*
—Steve Maraboli

WHAT?! Relationship to red lights? Who thinks like that? They're just red lights (or green or yellow). Who would even ask such a question?

My therapist. What does she know?

Apparently, a lot.

I was talking to her about this very book you are reading, and she asked me, "What do red lights mean to you?"

Hmmm. *Not sure, but I'll think about that and get back to you.* I cherish my therapist, and she's never led me astray. So, I stayed curious.

After setting the intention to discover how I relate to red lights, sure enough, I realized they were not neutral objects for me. In fact, red lights were a huge negative element. I did a lot of strategizing around not hitting them.

I'd watch for the countdown on the walk sign and gun it so I didn't have to sit at a red light. I would gun it after sitting at a red light so I didn't get the next red light.

Oh, the groan when I get *caught* by a red light!

How unproductive! The worst! In our super-productive culture, this was a negative. Sitting at a red light and not accomplishing anything. Horrendous!

Realizing my subconscious thinking about red lights, I decided to change that story. Maybe I could make this time "productive." Productive in mindfulness, becoming present.

So that is what I started to do. I would breathe and check into my body. Body-mind awareness. Remember that driving can be helpful to our physical, mental and spiritual health—or not. It's a choice.

Ahhh, time to put my nervous system consciously into rest, digest. Activate the parasympathetic nervous system. What a wonderful self-care this practice has been.

I started to look forward to red lights. Anticipating them and breathing, staying grounded and present.

To the dismay of people behind me, to be sure. I bet you have experienced racing through a yellow light, thinking, *Oh geez, I just made that,* and five cars behind you go through also. Am I disappointing those behind me? Maybe. Well, probably. I'll make sure to keep a few copies of this book and happily give them to those sitting behind me, giving me the finger, with angry looks on their faces. I'm sure I'll brighten their days.

Do I always feel grounded and peaceful when I stop? Nope. Sometimes I become aware of some anxiety, or the negative narrative going on in my head. And that's the point, to become aware—then I can make the choice to see what the anxiety may be about. What is true and not true about the negative thoughts.

Here is an example of a tension pattern that I've been curious about. Often, when I stop at a red light and check in for body tension, my left thigh is tense. So weird? Go ahead, lightly tighten your left upper leg. It's an isometric contraction of the hamstrings and quadriceps.

I have no idea what this is about and I don't really have to know. Did I see a snake to my left when I was camping at ten years old and tensed my left leg to get away? And then continued that pattern whenever I was scared there was a bug or something? Because that's how a lot of tension patterns happen. All done subconsciously. Until ... awareness is brought in and you can choose to relax the tension.

I have not gotten any insights into this pattern yet. I'll stay curious and endeavor not to be judgmental. This is just an example of staying present to *what is*.

The acceptance of the red light.

Say it, dear reader. "I accept red lights." How did that make you feel?

CHAPTER 10:

The Beauty of a Quieter Mind

"Such power there is in clear-eyed self-restraint."
—James Russell Lowell

MORE AND MORE, I catch myself getting into a story and easefully letting it go. This journey of becoming a more compassionate driver has been great training for being more mindful, grounded, and present.

Imagine you sent a text to someone and they didn't text back. You start to wonder why they are "ignoring" you, and your usual mental habit is to worry, get anxious about the way you may have come across .... And then you catch that train of thought and you let it go. You stop the charge in your nervous system, take a breath, and simply send another text asking for a response in a neutral way.

One small example, to be sure. Yet, they multiply. All the times my mind now stays quiet where once it was noisy feels so gratifying. I am so much more at peace with myself and the world around me in those moments.

As I mentioned in the beginning of this journey, my goal was to be kinder. Mostly while driving. Did it seep into other areas of my life? Absolutely!

Did I reach my goal of becoming a more mindful, kindful driver? Yes.

Has it helped me physically, mentally, and spiritually? Yes.

I'm still not a perfectly mindful and compassionate driver. Or person. I continually endeavor, though, to cultivate more mindfulness, more kindfulness, and ultimately more compassion—for myself and for all of humanity and nature.

If I can do it, so can you!

Know your why, and try, every time you are driving, to be the person who gives grace to others and to yourself.

When it doesn't work, and you end up toxic driving, simply spend some time reflecting—without judgment, because you give yourself grace and self-compassion. What would you want to do differently?

When you see other people toxic driving, send them grace and compassion.

Every now and then look at the whole of your life and ask yourself, "Is this mindful, kindful driving experience seeping into other aspects of my life?"

What does this self-compassion and more compassion for others feel like in your body? Want more of that?

Go ahead, where else can you take this capacity you are growing into?

Mindfulness, kindfulness can lead you down a big, deep hole—of compassion for all of humanity.

Remember, we're all in the same boat (this Earth boat) together. Remember, driving and road rage are universal shared experiences.

What if, even every now and then, you leave some grace and compassion in your wake on the road?

CHAPTER 11:

Various Valuable Techniques to Stop the Damn Stories and Steer You to the Highroad

AS I TALKED ABOUT in the first part of this book, my personal practices of yoga, martial arts, and meditation were extremely significant on this journey. More important was actually *applying* them to my highroad journey. Through these influences, I formulated the following techniques to become a more compassionate driver/human.

I offer you some of the techniques that were useful for me in this journey and which I continue to use. I'm getting better ...

Know Your Why—What You Want Most

I talked a lot about my "why" in Part II. For a healthier mind, body, and spirit and to feel more genuine. I would encourage you to find your why. If you read this far, I'm sure you have a why.

Here are some wise words from Bruce Kasanoff, whom I follow on LinkedIn because of his astute and sensible thoughts about self-awareness and self-discovery:

It is calming to ask yourself "What matters most?" on a regular basis. It is comforting. Enlightening. Why? Because the more often you ask yourself this question the more likely you are to have a life filled with what feeds your soul.

Breathe: Deep, Long, and Slow

Your breath is your best friend! Bringing your mind's attention to a long, slow, joyful, deep breath in, and a super-releasing, relaxing, letting-go exhale, will pull you into your center and into your inner environment. Now you can make a more conscious choice. Do three of these breaths and you change the part of the brain that deals with stress in a really good way.

Practicing breathing long, slow, and deep when *not* in a stressful situation is extremely useful. Think of it as training. Like training for a speech or a marathon. There needs to be repetitive practice before the big day. This is self-care training for those moments of stress.

Stop the Distractions (Mindlessness)

Stop multitasking. Putting on your mascara in the front window mirror while driving is dangerous. Taking your hands off the wheel and texting your friend back is dangerous, as we all know, so think, just this once.

I'm sure we all have turned the radio off or asked our passenger to wait to finish their story when we are lost or in an unfamiliar area. Why do we do that? Because the mind is not good at multitasking. Believe me, I researched this. If you are using your sense of sight to find where you are going, it's easier for your mind if it doesn't have to also use its sense of hearing.

Be strong enough to aim for present-moment awareness while driving. Meaning, stop doing more than driving while driving. You can do it!

Your Environment Matters

A clean car (home, office, desk) means a clear mind.

Your outer environment is as important as your inner environment. There is nothing peaceful and serene in a trashed-out car. It's worth your two minutes to declutter your car to feel good while driving. If you have kids, I feel for you. I now must work at keeping my car clean after the granddaughters have been in it. I learned the hard way, no crumbling cookies and definitely no chocolate.

Do a Dalai Lama—Leave Early for Your Appointments

The Dalai Lama was asked, "How do you stay so calm and peaceful all the time?"

To which he answered, "I leave early for my appointments."

So do a "Dalai Lama" and leave early!

There is a huge difference in my energy, my experience of driving when I'm not in a hurry.

Give this a try; make it a habit. Notice how your body and mind feel when you leave early. And when you're running late. Which feels better?

Understand What We Actually Have Control Of

Remembering what we have control of and letting go of what we don't is another simple concept, but not always easy to accomplish. Fact is, we don't have control over other drivers.

It really feels good when you don't let other drivers control you, your emotions, and yet letting go can be difficult. I agree! Remembering we don't have to let other drivers know what we think of their driving in our heads (a made-up story anyway) is great for your mind and body.

I printed the following words and hung them on a wall in my office. This list was a LinkedIn post by Jen Guidry. We cannot take all stupid-behaving drivers off the road. Since I can be one of them, I wouldn't be able to drive, either. When it really comes down to it, this can be one of my (our) biggest challenges.

Things you can control:
Your beliefs
Your attitudes
Your thoughts
Your perspective
How honest you are
Who your friends are
What books you read
How often you exercise
The type of food you eat
How many risks you take
How kind you are to others
How you interpret situations
How kind you are to yourself
How often you say "I love you"
How often you say "Thank you"
How you express your feelings
Whether or not you ask for help
How often you practice gratitude
How many times you smile today
The amount of effort you put forth
How you spend and invest your money
How much time you spend worrying

How often you think about the past

Whether or not you judge other people

Whether or not you try again after a setback

How much you appreciate the things you have

As you probably noticed, there is no mention of being able to control other drivers.

I hope this was helpful, dear reader, in many more ways than driving.

Emotional Freedom Technique—Tapping

Emotional Freedom Technique or EFT is also known as *tapping*. It was developed using the Chinese acupuncture meridians and points.

Tapping works because you are stimulating points on your body's energetic meridian systems. Ahhh, once again, science meets ancient wisdom (specifically acupuncture / Chinese medicine). Tapping on certain points can help to relieve symptoms such as stress, anxiety, cravings, and more.

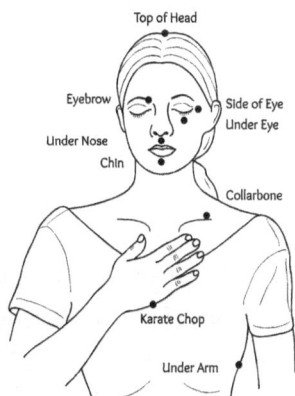

EFT Tapping Points

You can get a lot of information when doing a search on EFT (have fun) but I would like to share a truly simple way of how I use EFT when driving.

I stick to three points that you can tap on with one hand, by your collar bone. Using three fingers (which ones will vary for everyone) tap right under the left and right collar bone, the part closest to the throat. I use my thumb and fourth finger (you can also use your pinky finger). My ring finger taps right in between the two.

You can do this light, continuous tapping for thirty seconds to a few minutes when driving and you feel your body tensing. Whether due to traffic or really any time you would like to become calmer, more centered, and less tense. A calm body, a calm mind. And it is literally at your fingertips.

Be Aware of Our Emotional and Mental Patterns

Growing up and becoming a more aware human being is a worthy journey. Being able to see the emotional and mental tendencies that don't positively enhance your life is such a gift to yourself. Consider it self-care time. And really, this was, and is, the essence of my journey and this book.

We all harbor mental habits or tendencies that don't promote our health, that actually impede our growth into expanded awareness.

Use driving time to bring this awareness up. This, of course, is what we do when we become aware of a story. Take it a little further and find the patterns in the stories.

For example, one of the patterns that came up for me (if you haven't already figured it out) is I get really angry at people I deem selfish. "Selfish" was a word or a state my mother believed to be the absolute worst attribute a human being could have. I mean, it was really, really bad for us to be selfish.

Here's one story from my childhood that set up this pattern. When I was around five or six years old, I became anemic and needed to supplement with iron. For a while, I had to get my blood checked on a weekly basis. My mom would pack up all the kids and head to the doctor's office. I still remember that waiting room with the rows of big, dark brown chairs, playing among the chairs, and being silly with my other brothers and sisters. Then I would get called in to the doctor's room and sit on the end of the paper-covered bed to get one of my fingers pricked for my blood to be examined. The nurse was always so kind, asking me, "What finger do you want to use today?" Ahh, to have a choice as a child was such a wonderful thing.

When the nurse was done and she put a Band-Aid on my finger, she let me pick a piece of candy from the bowl. On this particular day, I decided I was going to bring some candy back for my siblings and started taking a few more. Here is what I heard my mother say to me, "Don't you dare be a selfish little girl. I won't have it! There is nothing worse in this world than being a selfish person."

Okay, what she most likely said was, "Connie, only one, we don't want to be selfish."

I felt small, like a bad girl, and horrified that my mother would think I was selfish. I'm not sure why I didn't tell her my reasoning behind my action, but I didn't. I just felt super admonished. Like most children, I didn't want to disappoint my mom.

The mental tendency that came from the consistent message from my mother to not be selfish was from childhood.

Another pattern I had for a few years was an anxiety pattern due to a car accident. Neither driver was hurt, thankfully, and I got the ticket because I was turning left at a red light and the other driver was going straight through the intersection. This accident caused me to doubt my driving skills a great deal. I tended to look three and four times to switch lanes or back out of a parking spot. I would catch myself saying things that were just plain silly and statistically improbable about what could have happened to me if ...

Three years after that accident, I was amazed and distraught that I was still making up drastic stories about what could be. One day, I got a lucky break. There was a therapist who had an office in the area where mine was and asked if I would be willing to help her get certified in Eye Movement Desensitization and Reprocessing (EMDR). She needed to have a few more preparation sessions to be fully certified. This is a technique to help with traumatic memories that are stuck and unprocessed. I told her about what was going on with my anxiety thoughts while driving due to the accident, and she said EMDR could be very helpful for me.

After two treatments, I caught myself backing out of a parking spot in a very busy area and only looking back twice. I literally said to myself, "That was just smart."

I am so grateful to be rid of that doubting myself habit pattern. If you have been in an accident and are having similar patterns, I suggest looking up EMDR practitioners in your area.

For now, bring awareness to any patterns that may come up, without judgment. Bring a sense of curiosity and open-mindedness. If you notice a pattern, you can choose to see what is under the pattern at a time that makes sense for you to take that deep dive. Kudos to you simply for being willing.

Anger—What Is Underneath It

The Greek philosophers say that anger is a *noble* emotion. Why? Because there is a lot of value in it for profound insights. If you take the time, energy, and courage to find what is underneath the anger, it can offer priceless understandings. Like the athletes who train their minds to not react impulsively to a negative situation, the road is our opportunity.

That being said, we can also consciously go back to a scenario and do a deeper dive into our reaction. This is not about making our anger wrong. It's about safety and our health.

When anger arises while you are driving—for whatever reason—decide to ask yourself, "What is under this anger? What could be the genuine reason I'm angry?" As I just mentioned, for me, the feeling that someone is selfish and inconsiderate (also, greedy, egotistical, thoughtless, pompous) grates on me. Currently, I am working on my over-giving and self-sacrificing, so this makes sense.

Even if you feel fully justified in being angry. For example, if someone recklessly cuts you off and endangers you and your children, you would have every reason to respond by cursing or acting aggressively.

Right?

Except it's not helpful.

If that were me in that scenario with my kiddos in the car, the underlying reason I would be angry at the driver is I have a need to keep my children safe.

Much of what I think you will find under the anger is an unmet need.

The need for safety.

The need to arrive to work on time.

The need to be relaxed.

The need to be seen and valued.

The need to live a fulfilling life.

The need for belonging.

Remember, anger can be the noblest of emotions if we follow

through to the underlying cause. And of course, this can take some time. Remember to also bring some levity to our human tendencies.

I am thankful that you made it this far on our journey together to become more kindful drivers and human beings. My heartful hope is that we are spreading a little bit more joy and compassion into this world, every day.

APPENDIX:
Mindfulness Practices

"Mindfulness is the only way out of the
past becoming your future."
—Jon Kabat-Zinn

WHAT ARE mindfulness practices?

Mindfulness practices are usually broken down into two categories, formal and informal.

Informal Practices

Informal practices are done in our day-to-day living.

They include mindful eating, mindful listening, bringing mindfulness to any of our body sensations. Listening, hearing, tasting, feeling (especially feeling our muscle tension).

Some examples of informal practices would be to mindfully make and eat one meal a day or week. Putting the fork down between each bite and really being aware of what you are eating, instead of scooping up and getting ready for your next bite. Many people have lost weight with just this one practice. We often don't realize how much or even what we are eating because we can be so lost in thought and habit.

Every single time you choose to notice your breath, or a sensation in the body, or the sights and sounds around you, you are becoming mindful to the moment.

That's because when you are aware of your body you are in the present moment. Body sensations can only be in the present. Unlike the mind, which can be lost in thought, in the future or the past.

If you have ever hit your finger instead of the nail with a hammer, you are completely present to that finger. You are not lost in thought or thinking about your to-do list.

Ways to Bring Mindfulness into Daily Living

These may seem simple and maybe even trite or boring, but give them a try. There are so many great benefits to not being on autopilot or lost in thoughts, especially thoughts which are harmful to yourself, to your health, and the health of your relationships.

Morning

1. Notice your first thoughts as you awake.
2. Make your coffee or tea slowly, gracefully, with much gratitude.
3. Brush your teeth, being fully present.
4. Put away your toothbrush with awareness.
5. Take time to sense the water of the shower on your body.
6. When shampooing your hair, give yourself a scalp massage.
7. Notice if there is any tension in your body as you get ready for the day.
8. Put on deodorant (notice the feel, the smell).
9. Pay meticulous attention to your shave.

10. Notice any tension in your face as you apply lotion/makeup.
11. Notice your hunger or non-hunger.
12. Slow down eating breakfast.
13. Take a few moments to step outside and breathe.
14. Notice the feeling of putting on your shoes.
15. Wait at the door an extra moment to see if there is anything you need for the day.
16. Drink water, noticing the temperature and the liquid sensation.

Going to Work, Being at Work

1. Sit for a moment before starting the car. How does your body feel?
2. Notice if the car smells (or not).
3. Drive with the radio off and notice your thoughts. No judgment; it's about awareness and choice—to continue the thought or let it go.
4. Take a deep, grateful breath ... then start your day.
5. Eat lunch with little to no distractions, with the intent to fully enjoy your food.
6. Check in three times throughout the day for any tension that may be in your body. Let the tension go and smile.

Evening

1. Before entering your home, notice your posture.
2. Check in with your thoughts about what the evening holds.
3. Check in with your body, with your energy level. No judgment; simple awareness.

4. Take long, slow inhales and exhales as you cook dinner, eat dinner.
5. Bring awareness to your external environment. What do you sense?
6. Notice your breath as you change into your night clothes.
7. Make choices that allow your body to relax and get ready for sleep.
8. Think about those things that you're grateful for. What happens to your body?

Formal Practices

Formal practices are done for a certain amount of time away from day-to-day activities.

They include: seated meditation, walking meditation, yoga, tai chi, and I have even seen classes called mindful dancing.

Here is a simple formal meditation practice you can do right now if you have a few minutes.

Sit comfortably. If on a cushion, cross your legs comfortably in front of you. If on a chair, rest the bottoms of your feet on the floor. Eyes can be closed, or you can gaze at some point downward. Body should feel relaxed and attentive, regal even.

Feel your breath. Bring your attention to the physical sensation of breathing: the air moving through your nose or mouth, the rising and falling of your belly, the expansion and contraction of your rib cage.

Notice when your mind wanders from your breath. Inevitably, your attention will leave the breath and wander to other places. Don't worry. There's no need to block or eliminate thinking. When you notice your mind wandering, gently return your attention to the breath.

Be kind about your wandering mind. You may find your mind wandering constantly—that's normal, too. Instead of wrestling with your thoughts, practice observing them without reacting. Just sit and pay attention. As hard as it is to maintain, that's all there is. Come back to your breath repeatedly, without judgment or expectation. That moment when you become aware that you are somewhere else is a magical moment.

When you are ready, gently lift your gaze (if your eyes are closed, open them). Take a moment and notice any sounds in the environment. Notice how your body feels right now. Notice your thoughts and emotions.

Mindfulness Body Scan Meditation

The following is a fifteen-minute, formal mindfulness meditation to bring you into your body and become completely present. When you are "in" your body, aware of your body, you begin the process of becoming present to the moment.

When I took my first course in mindfulness, we were instructed to do certain exercises. One of them was to listen to a body scan meditation five times per week. It was forty-five minutes! I can't tell you how I fought this. Forty-five minutes out of my day! But I did it.

Each time I was finished, I felt like my body was buzzing. Like my body was so alive. I was always glad I took that time. So, here is a version that I think you will enjoy in the same way, just a bit shorter.

Journaling Questions

What is your biggest WHY? Why do you want to speed toward compassion?

What makes you the angriest when driving?

You are coming up to an intersection and you know the light is most likely going to turn yellow by the time you get close. What are you thinking?

Think about a time when you were inconvenienced. How did you respond?

What does having to stop at a red light mean to you?

What are your needs when it comes to driving?

How can you meet these needs when you are driving?

How do you handle "stupid" drivers? Or how would you *like* to handle "stupid" drivers?

What gets in the way of you enjoying driving?

What is your relationship to a quiet, still, mind? Is there any fear there?

Do you believe you have innate kindness? If so, how does this show up for you when driving?

When do you feel most genuine and authentically you?

We all have an inner critic. How do you catch yours, and how would you like to deal with this?

Are you good at knowing what your needs are? What are some of your needs?

If not, would you be willing to spend time with your feelings, especially your anger, to see what is underneath?

What's right about being rageful on the road? (Sometimes, asking the question with "what's right" about something we feel negative about brings up interesting awarenesses.)

Can you think of a tension or habitual pattern you may have generated from imitating other adults? Are they patterns you want to keep?

ENDNOTES

Chapter 2

"You may indeed exemplify kindness..." Wayne Dyer, *Being in Balance: 9 Principles for Creating Habits to Match* (Carlsbad, CA: Hay House, 2006), 52.

"There is nothing wrong with anger as an emotion..." Stan Steindl, James Kirby, "Road Rage: Why Normal People become harmful on the Roads," Psychology Consultants, August 8, 2016, https://psychologyconsultants.com.au/ road-rage-why-normal-people-become-harmful-on-the-roads/.

Chapter 3

"I don't think people are really seeking..." Joseph Campbell, *The Power of Myth*, with Bill Moyers (New York: Doubleday, 1988), 120.

The Enneagram: Don Richard Riso and Russ Hudson, *The Wisdom of the Enneagram*, (New York: Bantam Books, 1999), pp 355-356.

Chapter 4
Definition of dogmatism: Maryam Malmir, Mohammad Khanahmadi, and Darjush Farhud, "Dogmatism and Happiness," *Iranian Journal of Public Health* 46, no. 3 (March 2017), https://www.ncbi.nlm.nih.gov/pmc/articles/PMC5395528/.

Chapter 5
Rhea Powers, *Unfolding the Soul: 90 Day Program to Understanding Your Inner Critic*, (Accessible Publishing Systems, 2015), #21.

Nick Cave on the soul: "I Love the Song Night Raid," The Red Hand Files, Issue #216, December 2022, https://www.theredhand-files.com/i-love-the-song-night-raid/.

Chapter 6
Brené Brown, *The Gifts of Imperfection* (Center City, MN: Hazelden Publishing, 2010), 74.

Kristin Neff quoted in: "The Power of Self-Compassion," *Greater Good Magazine*, March 4, 2012, Greatergood.berkeley.edu/article/item/the_power_of_self-compassion.

Mindfulness definition from *Psychology Today*: accessed January 25, 2024, https://www.psychologytoday.com/intl/basics/mindfulness.

Chapter 7
"The need to make up a story…" Brené Brown, *Rising Strong: How the Ability to Reset Transforms the Way We Live, Love. Parent, and Lead* (New York: Random House, 2017), 79.

Chapter 11
Bruce Kasanoff, "My Best Lessons From a Decade of Ghostwriting," LinkedIn, April 18, 2022, https://www.linkedin.com/pulse/my-best-lessons-from-decade-ghostwriting-bruce-kasanoff/.

Jen Guidry, "Things We Can Control," BrilliantlyBold.com, January 2023, https://1faithfulwarrior.com/2023/01/21/things-we-can-control/, January 2023.

ACKNOWLEDGMENTS

I WANT TO HONOR AND GIVE THANKS to the many people who know me and helped me through this process.

Much gratitude and love to Brett Warden for his unwavering belief in me and this book. My belief and faith were not unwavering.

Gratitude to my children, Kurt and Alexis, for not only helping me grow my capacity as a parent and human being but also for your sense of humor and letting me enjoy life with you as adults.

Gratitude to My Word Publishing for their support and navigating me through the whole book writing process. Specifically, thank you to editor Alexandra O'Connell for keeping me on task, for great editing, and for sharing your sense of humor. Also, to K. B. Jensen of My Word Publishing, for coaching me through this process in a way that stayed true to my genuine self.

Much gratitude to Fran Gallaher for her insights and spiritual wisdom. You get me. Special gratitude to Carolyn Rice Young for the three decades of wise teaching in the Luminous Ladies spiritual group.

And, of course, great gratitude to all the beautiful Luminous Ladies in that group. Much gratitude to Larisa Gerace for her friendship and another discoverer of Life-as-a-Teacher and being a go-to safe person when I need to be vulnerable. Thank you, Keith Renninsen and Alexis Warden, for being so kind with your valuable feedback reading the drafts of this book.

I also want to honor and give thanks to those who don't know me but helped me with their books and podcasts, with their courage to be vulnerable, and their wisdom. To Brené Brown, Tara Brach, Jack Kornfield, Mark Nepo, Jai Dav, Christina L. Pratt, and many others ... there really are too many to mention. Also, to Jesse Itzler for his book *Living with the Monks*. Your humorous writing style and quest convinced me to finish this book at a time I didn't think I would.

ABOUT THE AUTHOR

CONNIE WARDEN is a compulsive discoverer of all things expanding our human potential. She is an acupuncturist and has a masters in oriental medicine. Connie has been a yoga student for forty years and a teacher for twenty. Her diverse mindfulness trainings help her lead varied meditation practices. She is currently living in Colorado with her husband and two cats, Buffy and Lucky (who love to sit on her keyboard when she is writing).

You can visit her website at ConnieWarden.com.